# MANAGERIAL ACCOUNTING ACTIVITIES



**Neal J. Hannon**

Bryant College

South-Western College Publishing

Thomson Learning™

Australia • Canada • Denmark • Japan • Mexico • New Zealand • Philippines

Puerto Rico • Singapore • South Africa • Spain • United Kingdom • United States

Managerial Accounting Activities by Hannon
Acquisitions Editor: Rochelle Kronzek
Developmental Coordinator: Megan Smith-Creed
Marketing Manager: Matt Filimonov
Production Editor: Marci Dechter
Manufacturing Coordinator: Doug Wilke
Cover Design: Rick Moore
Cover Photographer or Illustrator: Susan LeVan/ ©1997, Artville, LLC
Printer: Webcom



Printed in Canada
1 2 3 4 5 02 01 00 99

For more information contact South-Western College Publishing, 5101 Madison Road, Cincinnati, Ohio, 45227 or find us on the Internet at http://www.swcollege.com



ISBN: 0-324-02012-0

This book is printed on acid-free paper.

# Contents

# Preface

The purpose of this workbook is to provide students with real-world examples of managerial accounting situations. Students will be challenged to utilize managerial accounting skills by developing comprehensive responses to case study situations. Students will communicate their answers while developing skills in report writing, presentation preparation and delivery, using the Internet, and improving analytical skills. The focus of the cases is the primary concepts of management accounting.

### *Why Managerial Accountants Need Additional Skills*

Management needs information to make decisions. The information needed usually takes the form of data extracted from databases fed by accounting and other information systems. Management accountants are responsible for the integrity of the inputs to outputs of a company's accounting system. Traditionally, management accountants have been asked to provide management with answers to questions relating to where the figures came from and what changes they need to make to see an improvement in the numbers. The scorecard for management becomes the information developed by management accountants from the managerial control system. Management accountants are in an ideal position to provide that information.

Employees today are being asked to prepare financial information for management, and to participate in the discovery of the underlying problems and in the implementation of solutions.

The skills required of employees to become valuable members of financial teams is changing rapidly. No longer is it sufficient to just assemble reports and compile numbers. Today's accountants and financial professionals need to be multi-dimensional team players, contributing to overall company performance. They need to acquire skills in communication on several dimensions, including face-to-face dialogue, group meetings, oral and written presentations, and electronic communications.

Here's a sample of what people are saying about the new accounting/financial graduate and the skills he/she will need to possess:

- *Strong oral and written communications skills are a must. The ability to compose letters, detailed financial reports, and memos to executives and other colleagues will help set you apart. Those skills have not been part of the traditional accounting requirements until now. ...Today's team-oriented finance department has placed an increased focus on interpersonal and communications skills. Cross-functional work teams are gaining favor as a way to improve customer service and increase productivity.*

Max Messmer, chairman and chief executive officer at Robert Half International writing for the Institute of Management Accounting's student home page located at http://www.rutgers.edu/Accounting/raw/ima/students/messmer.html, September 1998.

- *Companies want people who can explain the implications of the financial data they are presenting. They want people who can bring their finance experience to bear in a cross-functional team or environment. This requires communication skills, an understanding of the overall business process, and the ability to explain financial information to the rest of the company.*

Ann Moncus, a partner with Arthur Anderson in San Francisco. Quote taken from *Controller Magazine*, September 1997, page 10.

- *We believe that clear writing equals clear thinking and that prospective employers are expecting new graduates to have a broader array of skills than ever before. It's vital that our students know how to communicate effectively as well as be technically proficient in the nuts and bolts of financial reporting.*

Professor Daniel W. Collins, Henry B. Tippie Research Chair in Accounting at the University of Iowa.

- *BUSINESS RELIANCE ON THE INTERNET WILL JUMP OVER 500% BY 1999*

  *NEW YORK – April 9, 1997 – The share of major U.S. firms heavily reliant on the Internet will increase over 500 percent by 1999, according to a study released today by the American Management Association (AMA) and Philadelphia strategic communications agency Tierney & Partners. The survey is the largest to date on Internet use for business purposes.*

  *Six percent of surveyed businesses say they are "heavy" users of the Internet today, the study found, but that figure will increase to 38 percent by 1999 – a 533 percent increase.*

  *An assessment of current and future Internet use by nearly 3,500 executives and managers found that 64 percent make some use of the Internet from their offices today, averaging 3.1 hours per week, and only three percent are on-line for 10 or more hours weekly.*

*However, by 1999, the survey found, 82 percent will use the Internet, at an average 7.9 hours per week, and 24 percent will be on-line for 10 or more hours weekly – a 700 percent increase in "heavy" users, as defined by AMA and Tierney & Partners.*

Taken from an American Management Association press release. Found at http://www.amanet.org/survey/netrel.htm

- *The basic content of the (CPA) exam is undergoing intense scrutiny. The adjustments are necessary because of the changing nature of the accounting industry.*

"Reengineering the CPA Exam," Mike Walker, CPA and chair of the Board of Examiners (BOE), an 11-member American Institute of Certified Public Accountants (AICPA) group at the American Accounting Association Conference (AAA) in New Orleans, August 1998.

- *We should place more emphasis on information technology. Secondly, it (the findings) said we should spend more time and testing on general business knowledge, more on the big picture, understanding the business environment...understanding issues and their implications and more testing of the applications of skills – communication skills, analytic, research, consulting and critical thinking.*

David Pearson, Ernst & Young, a member and future chair of the Content Oversight Task Force formed in 1996 ago by AAA. David was referring to the findings accumulated from extensive feedback from the nation's experts on accounting.

- *What Is The New Finance?*

  *The New Finance is a term coined by the AICPA's Management Accounting Executive Committee (now called the Business and Industry Executive Committee) to describe the revolutionary changes that have taken place globally in financial management in the last decade. The New Finance encompasses hard-core management accounting topics like: cost management (ABC, target costing, etc.), cash flows, discount rates, capacity management etc; manufacturing issues like just-in-time production, distribution channels management, competitive intelligence, etc., to softer topics like benchmarking, performance measurement, cross-functional teams, managing change, etc. In summary, The New Finance is less about accounting and more about management – and becoming strategic decision-makers in our companies.*

Taken from the AICPA's Web site, www.aicpa.org, September 17, 1998.

- *For many firms, designing and implementing a proactive competitive intelligence process represents a major shift in focus. The organization must move from emphasizing historical, financial, internally oriented information toward an externally oriented view emphasizing the market, market forces, and competitors. Creating such a shift must start with top management and be reinforced continually by those managers. For CPAs, the challenge is to apply to this new area their ability to think strategically and their skills in data gathering, analysis and presentation.*

Taken from the AICPA's Web site, www.aicpa.org, September 17, 1998.

- *With products, partners and processes constantly changing, you'll also need to become more flexible and change-oriented. Working in teams, you'll need to become skilled in group processes, facilitation and co-ordination. "Communication skills, including speaking, writing, listening, and reading, will be vital," says Tony Jackson, controller of the Atlanta Committee for the 1996 Olympic Games. So will interpersonal skills and the ability to form relationships.*

Shari Caudron, "Finance in the Next Millennium," *Controller Magazine*, January 1997.

- *Running a report to print on a piece of paper is one of the most wasteful tasks that an accounting department can do. Reports are a repository of much useful information about the business – information that special report "mining" tools can make great use of. Report-mining software can interrogate this information and take action by utilizing the business rules stored in your company's own knowledge base.*

Stewart McKie, "Visionary Accounting," *Controller Magazine*, January 1997.

- *Carrier's complexity reduction process has evolved into a formal, systematic program with corporate-wide visibility. The cost of complexity (COC) programs are administrated at the plant level by COC teams. COC teams are formed by recruiting mid-level managers from each functional area including manufacturing, engineering, accounting, and materials management. Once a team is formed, it documents its goals, objectives, and deliverables. It then agrees to a methodology for financially evaluating complexity costs and potential cost reduction opportunities. ... Carrier considers this program to be one of its critical success factors.*

Dan W. Swenson, "Managing Costs through Complexity Reduction at Carrier Corporation," *Management Accounting*, April 1998.

- *About the only thing we can do by not keeping up with the times is to look like luddites to our students who are whizzing around our best thoroughbreds in their new Model Ts. In a sense we can also hurt our students by not having curricula that adapt to changing technology conditions in their careers and their lives in the 21st Century.*

Written by Professor Robert E. Jensen, Jesse H. Jones Distinguished Professor of Business Administration Trinity University, in a posting to the AECM discussion list (Accounting Education using Computers and Multimedia <AECM@VAX.LOYOLA.EDU>), September 21, 1998.

Traditional and contemporary management accounting texts focus on gathering data and preparing reports. In other words, they focus on the mechanics of assembling information. Although this is a critical part of a financial professional's job, it only addresses about 20 percent of the job focus of today's job responsibilities. Current textbook material places little if any significance on the tasks that make up 80 percent of a typical financial professional's job. Those missing job tasks include the distribution, interpretation, and assimilation of financial information. This is a major oversight.

For over 15 years in the practice of management accounting, well over half my time was spent in distributing information and explaining information to various members of the management team. Daily meetings with operation department heads, weekly meetings with middle management, monthly meetings with the bosses – all had several things in common. The people wanted information they could use to make decisions and they wanted it quickly. Also, the reports developed by the finance department often came up short of what was really needed to make decisions. The reports often gave an accurate history of past events while providing no insight into how to either make corrections or to make improvements in the future.

The information was normally organized in isolation of the collective decisions that created it. For example, an increase in engineering spending was reported as an engineering variance to budget, not as a potential overrun or delay on a critical project. An overtime spending report, organized by a supervisor, provided no clues as to why the overtime was incurred. Typical managerial accounting reports came out too late to be of use for decision making.

## *What's Different Today*

Businesses are beginning to take a new approach to using management accounting information. Businesses are using internal networks, or Intranets, to speed information to everyone who needs the information when the information is available. Today's computer systems are permitting cross-functional teams to receive accurate, up-to-the-minute reports on all aspects of their projects from spending to schedule. Managers are using online databases to pull down customized reports that better suit their needs and they have access to the information, in some cases, 24 hours per day, 7 days per week. Virtual team rooms are being established where team members can hold meetings, post new information, make decisions and more without ever leaving their computers.

Management accountants need to know how to best serve this new environment. They need to be able to quickly respond, online, to the organization's need for targeted information and be prepared to explain to everybody what the information means. They need to post critical data to Intranets quickly and efficiently. They need to post team data for internal team distribution. They need to be available via e-mail, in a discussion group, or in a departmental chat room to answer questions relating to both financial information and strategic direction.

The New Finance is all about using the base of a sound understanding of financial information to make solid management team contributions that go well beyond simply dumping off the numbers. The New Finance involves understanding the big picture of where a company is heading and what it is attempting to accomplish. Using this deeper understanding, finance professionals will be able to give guidance and direction to the management team, as they demand more and more information, and demand it more quickly. Making decisions more quickly, due to access to information on a more timely basis, will not in itself result in better decisions. The entire management team needs to lean on the insights of modern financial professionals for direction and guidance.

This book will provide professors with the tools to introduce students to the new world of finance. Using real-world examples and situations, students will be asked to prepare reports, give oral presentations, post information electronically, interpret the "big picture," and become active team members of cross-disciplined teams. Students will get a taste of the 80 percent side of a financial professional's job while picking up valuable business skills. Professors will gain material to introduce oral and written communication skills, teamwork exercises, real-world applications for electronic distribution of information, and valuable hints on how to make the exercises realistic and rewarding.

# Chapter 1

# Allocation of Costs

Management expert Peter Drucker makes a simple case for management accounting while writing in the *Wall Street Journal.*[1] He states that business executives are information literate, meaning they know how to gather data. They do not know, however, how to ask the right questions to get the information they need to get their job done. As our economy moves increasingly from producing goods and services to producing information, the need for all business people to get the right information will increase. According to Drucker, "The challenges increasingly will not be technical, but to convert data to usable information that is actually being used."[2]

The following situations will give you the opportunity to begin understanding what information is important and how to use that information to help management make informed decisions.

## *Assignment 1-A: Opening Story: All Sports Facility*

All Sports Facility, Inc. (ASF), a new recreational resource area focusing on the physical development needs of persons between the ages of 18 through 40, has just opened in Plymouth, Massachusetts, 15 miles south of Boston. The facility has several basketball courts, sand pits for beach volleyball, an indoor soccer field, batting cages, a golf ball hitting area, and a rink for floor hockey. A large dining room is located inside the building with ample windows for viewing the action below. In addition to establishing house leagues, ASF hopes to attract large parties and gatherings for corporate events. The facility can accommodate up to 1,000 people at a time.

Regular maintenance expense items include additional sand for the pits, baseball bats and balls, spare parts for the baseball pitching machine, and sweepers for the indoor soccer surface. Additional maintenance expenses include floor buffing equipment, basketballs and nets, replacement sections for the boards in the floor hockey arena, and locker room repairs. Common expenses include insurance for the building and the parking lot; advertising; city property taxes; and utility, phone, and Internet connection charges.

The management team at ASF consists of three recent graduates majoring in recreational education from a local university, a financial officer, a building and grounds manager, a salesperson, and a general manager. The ASF team meets every day for one hour to

---

[1] From P. Drucker, "Be Data Literate—Know What to Know," *The Wall Street Journal*, December 1, 1992, p.14.
[2] Ibid.

discuss all business matters that concern the company. The subject of cost allocation has come become a main topic at these meetings.

Samantha, one of the recreational experts, is concerned about the pricing for the volleyball leagues. How much should they charge per team? What about cancellation charges? What about insurance? Should an insurance charge be added to the league fee or should the insurance costs be allocated and charged as overhead? ASF pays a liability insurance charge of $25,000 per year and extra charges for each organized league it runs. The team's decision on this matter could mean the difference between having a successful initial season or not attracting enough players for league play.

1) What information will be needed to determine the nature of the costs described? How should the team decide which costs are fixed and which are variable?

2) What contributions should the team expect from each of its team members on the cost allocation question? Can you suggest a structure for the team meeting that might help the members reach a reasonable conclusion?

3) What should the financial officer be concerned about when it comes to deciding on cost allocations? What about the buildings and grounds manager? Should he be concerned about cost allocations? What should the salesperson bring to this discussion?

4) What information will the team need prior to making any decisions? How can information be developed for areas where no historical information presently exists?

5) Marty, the salesperson, states that a similar business located 70 miles to the north charges each person a $100 membership fee plus league fees. League fees for volleyball amount to $1,200 per team for a 15-week season, including playoffs. How could this information be used to help the allocation question? If the information was presented in a meeting, how should the team handle the input?

### *Cost Accumulations*

Spending money is easy. Companies, like individuals, have great capacity to spend cash. Keeping track of dollars spent is also easy provided a good accounting system is in place. What is difficult for companies is to develop meaningful accounts for cost collection and then distribute the costs to the products and services sold to customers in a fair and equitable manor. The process of accumulating and then allocating costs to products and services is a major part of management accounting.

### *Assignment 1-B: Case Study: Solectria Corporation*

Solectria Corporation is a private company that manufactures electric automobiles. Worldwide sales of electric vehicles will number in the thousands in 1999, compared to over 20 million in sales of gasoline-powered cars. Solectria normally purchases gas-powered cars, typically Chevy Metros, and refurbishes the cars to run on electric components. The selling price for the altered vehicles, called Solectria Force electric sedans, was $34,000 in 1998.

Karl Thidemann, director of marketing for the company, recently negotiated a deal with General Motors where GM would send Solectria automobile chassis, less the gas engines, directly to the company. Because of the savings, Solectria is now able to reduce 1999 prices to $26,000.

1) What changes are required in the accounting system to account for the lower initial price paid for the car and the lower amounts of labor required for the conversion?

_______________________________________________

_______________________________________________

_______________________________________________

_______________________________________________

_______________________________________________

_______________________________________________

_______________________________________________

_______________________________________________

_______________________________________________

2) What changes in the allocation methods need to be made?

_______________________________________________

_______________________________________________

_______________________________________________

_______________________________________________

_______________________________________________

_______________________________________________

_______________________________________________

_______________________________________________

_______________________________________________

In a recent press release, Mark Kopec, executive vice president, said "Increased sales of the popular Solectria Force electric sedan are being driven by a significant price cut in the 1999 model, made possible by our just-announced chassis deal with a major auto company. We also see significant growth in new sales of our more powerful drive systems to manufacturers of buses, trucks, and other industrial vehicles over the next few months, both in the US and abroad."[3]

Another product recently introduced by the company is the Sunrise. The Sunrise is a sporty car built from the ground up with composite materials. Using one-piece body construction, the metal-free car allows approximately twice the range as the standard Solectria automobile. Virtually made by hand, the Sunrise sells for a price close to $200,000. Thidemann is currently in negotiations with a major automotive producer to

---

[3] Karl Thiedemann, "Solectria Reports Strong Sales," December, 8, 1998; http://www.solectria.com/strongsale.html

bring the volume of Sunrise cars manufactured up to 20,000 per year. At that level, the cost structure would change significantly.

3) What elements of the cost structure are likely to change if the manufactured volume of the Sunrise jumps from 15 per year to 20,000?

_______________________________________________________________

_______________________________________________________________

_______________________________________________________________

_______________________________________________________________

_______________________________________________________________

_______________________________________________________________

_______________________________________________________________

Visit the main Solectria Web site at http://www.solectria.com/

### *Assignment 1-C: Case Study: Hannon's Tastee Freeze Soft-Serve Ice Cream*

Back in 1963, Jack Hannon owned a soft-serve ice cream store on a busy highway. The menu was very simple. Ice cream cones, sundaes, soft drinks, and milkshakes were 95 percent of sales. Ice cream cones came in five sizes that began at $.05 and topped off at $.25. Regular sundaes cost $.35. Big spenders could purchase a banana split for $.50. A good day saw revenue exceed $100, with typical monthly sales reaching $3,200. Two ice cream machines were used to make the soft-serve ice cream.

Each week, Jack offered a weekly special sundae for $.20. Depending on the popularity of the flavor of the sundae, the weekly special could increase total sales revenue. On the special occasion when the best seller, hot fudge sundae, was offered, the lines outside the store would remain five people deep at each sales window all week long. People would ask Jack how he could sell a hot fudge sundae for $.20 and make any money. He would just laugh and say something about all the cars in the parking lot.

What went into a hot fudge sundae? The component costs include four ounces of soft-serve ice cream costing $.04; 1.5 ounces of hot fudge costing $.08; a plastic bowl, plastic spoon, and two napkins (on average) costing $.02 altogether; and about two minutes of labor to take the order, prepare the sundae, serve, and make change, costing $.03. Other costs to run the business included electricity, rent for the building, insurance, permit costs, cleaning supplies, and cleaning labor. These other costs typically cost $1,075 per month.

What did Jack Hannon know about the nature of fixed and variable costs? What were the components of cost for the Hannon hot fudge sundae? Did Hannon's Tastee Freeze make any money on the hot fudge special?

1) How would you define the relevant range for Hannon's Tastee Freeze?

2) Which costs are variable in the sale of a sundae?

3) If a $.20 soft-serve ice cream cone has five ounces of ice cream costing $.05, a cone costing $.02, and labor costing $.03, how much money does the sale of one cone contribute to gross margin?

4) Given the profitability of the ice cream cones and sundaes at normal prices, why would Hannon's Tastee Freeze sell a weekly special for $.20?

5) From time to time, Jack would take a shift selling ice cream. As the owner, Jack would not pay himself an hourly wage. When Jack was working, what effect did his actions have on variable costs? Did this action have an effect on total product costs? Why or why not?

### *Assignment 1-D: Team Project: Hannon's Tastee Freeze*

**Details:** Develop a day's worth of sales and costs for Hannon's Tastee Freeze. Make assumptions for the number of sundaes to be sold at \$.20 and \$.35, ice cream cones sold at the \$.05, \$.10, \$.15, \$.20, and \$.25 levels, and banana splits sold at \$.50 (assume that the splits are the equivalent of two sundaes plus \$.05 worth of bananas). Total sales for the day should be \$100.

**Assignments:** Split the team into sales and cost groups. The sales group will work on the number of units that need to be sold to reach the sales target and the cost group will work on costing the sales forecast. Show projected income statement for the day's sales. Hint: Don't forget to add in the fixed costs for one day.

**Analysis:** What actions could be taken to increase the profits for any given day? What are the elements of cost that are under the control of the management of the business? How could the actual products sold affect how much profit can be made on a given day? Include a summary of the profit potential for each major sales item.

**Report:** Prepare a slide presentation to the owner of Hannon's Tastee Freeze detailing the analysis from the above question. If time permits, present your group's findings to the class in a ten-minute or less oral and slide presentation.

## *Assignment 1-E: Using Spreadsheets: Hannon's Tastee Freeze*

The development of strong analytical skills is an important part of the management accountant's job. Throughout this skills book, examples of using numbers and spreadsheets to contribute to the understanding of financial information will be presented. Develop a spreadsheet in either Lotus™ or Excel™ for calculating the standard cost for a $.25 soft-serve ice cream cone. Use the information provided in Assignment 1-C. Write a short paragraph explaining all formulas developed for your spreadsheet and explain how parts of this spreadsheet might be used in developing standard costs for the other sizes of soft-serve ice cream cones. The assignment should include a printout of your spreadsheet and a copy of the file on disk to be handed in to the instructor.

# Chapter 2

## Standard Costs and Job Order Costing

Determining the cost of an item is never a simple task. Accountants have developed several methods for accomplishing this task, including standard costing, job order costing, and activity-based costing. Standard costs and job order costs are addressed in this chapter. Activity-based costs will be discussed in Chapter 3.

Standard costs are commonly used for determining product costs where manufacturing processes are predictable and repeatable. A standard cost seeks to determine what a product should cost and then provides the tools to determine the difference between the predicted (standard) cost and the actual cost of a product. In most traditional systems, costs are determined first by identifying spending on resources that will be converted into products for sale. Those resources normally consist of raw materials. Next, functional areas add value to the resources creating products and services sold.

Functional areas spend money in order to complete the resource conversion. For example, a building contractor might have a department for building foundations. When a foundation is laid, construction workers are needed to run the equipment. Both the raw materials, most likely concrete and steel, and the wages for the construction workers are spent in the transformation process of taking a vacant lot and turning it into a building foundation.

The spending by functional area, such as the building foundation department above, is applied to the products and services sold. The main premise is that companies will have to spend money to obtain resources and to make value-added conversions such as a vacant lot to a poured foundation. Customers, when the job is complete, will pay for the value added to the lot. If the value added by the company making the resource conversion is great enough, customers for the products and services will pay money in excess of the costs paid by the company.

The standard cost for the building foundation above is the amount of raw material, labor, and other costs it should take to complete the foundation. A job order cost would include all the elements of the above but would collect actual costs charged to the job instead of standard cost. In other words, if the raw material for concrete had a standard cost of $15,000 but actually cost $15,750, a job costing system would charge $15,750 to the job. A standard cost system would charge $15,000 to the job and write off the extra $750 to a variance account.

## *Assignment 2-A: Opening Story: Pizza Mia*

Let's look at the costs associated with a local pizza store, Pizza Mia. Pizza consists of dough, sauce, various meat and vegetable toppings, and cheese. When properly prepared and cooked, the result is a tasty, complete meal. Successful pizza shops like Pizza Mia will create great tasting pizza that can be sold at a price that exceeds the cost to make the pizza. Like snowflakes, no two pizzas are exactly alike. Slight differences in the amount of cheese used, the number of pepperoni slices, mushrooms, etc., can all vary. How then, can the owner of a pizza shop ever know what his/her costs are?

To determine the cost of each pizza, a standard must be developed. This standard, or uniform method, measures the average amount of ingredients that *should* be used in the making of each pizza. The standard might also specify how many, on average, mushrooms it takes to make a mushroom pizza. Each pizza is likely to carry a different number of mushrooms. The actual number of mushrooms will most likely be different from the average. Short of counting each mushroom on each pizza, most cost systems will use the average number of mushrooms as the basis for calculating the mushroom portion of the standard cost.

In addition to the cost of the mushrooms, the material portion of the standard cost would include the pizza dough, the sauce, the cheese and other toppings, and the delivery box. Labor costs would include the wages paid to the pizza makers and the delivery people. Overhead would include the cost to keep the ovens running, the utility expenses, the rent of the building, and the cost of management salaries. Overhead would also include insurance, taxes, and any license fees paid to local governments.

Once the overhead costs have been accumulated, the next major task is to determine how to distribute the overhead back to the products. The big question is how much overhead should be allocated or charged to each pizza? The method chosen by management for the distribution of overhead costs to products is the heart of the standard cost decision. In the next two cases, think about how each company allocates overhead.

1) What are the main components of the standard cost of the pizza? How should they be determined?

______________________________________________________________________

______________________________________________________________________

______________________________________________________________________

______________________________________________________________________

______________________________________________________________________

______________________________________________________________________

2) How much labor should go into the standard cost of a pizza? What method would you suggest to Pizza Mia to measure the labor costs per pizza sold?

_______________________________________________

_______________________________________________

_______________________________________________

_______________________________________________

_______________________________________________

3) What impact does cooking time in the oven for each pizza have on the standard cost?

_______________________________________________

_______________________________________________

_______________________________________________

_______________________________________________

_______________________________________________

4) What costs should not go into the makeup of the standard cost of making pizzas? Hint: Costs that are included in a standard cost are *should* costs.

_______________________________________________

_______________________________________________

_______________________________________________

_______________________________________________

_______________________________________________

5) How should overhead be allocated to each pizza? Identify two methods for overhead allocation that Pizza Mia should consider. Which method do you recommend here?

_______________________________________________

_______________________________________________

_______________________________________________

_______________________________________________

_______________________________________________

_______________________________________________

_______________________________________________

_______________________________________________

6) Suppose a customer orders a pizza that is not on the menu and for which a standard has not yet been determined. Can you suggest a method for handling the costing of a non-standard pizza?

________________________________________________________________

________________________________________________________________

________________________________________________________________

________________________________________________________________

________________________________________________________________

________________________________________________________________

________________________________________________________________

________________________________________________________________

### *Assignment 2-B: Case Study: The Impossible Standard*

The phone rang early, around 7:15 a.m. It was Jennifer, the work team leader of the circuit board testing group. Jennifer was in desperate need of information and fast. Jennifer's boss, the manager of testing, had dropped off a report detailing the circuit board testing team's recent performance. To say the least, the report was not good. In fact, the report indicated that the testing group's output was well below standard. In this situation, Jason's job is to help Jennifer understand the report and to suggest actions her group can take to improve.

Jennifer said, "Jason, what's up with this report? Your reports always put us in a bad light. We are working very hard and all we get is criticized for our efforts. What do you suggest?" Jason thought a second and then responded. "Jennifer, have you looked at the details of the report? It shows the individual jobs your group has tested in the last week, the amount of time allowed for each test (the standard time in minutes), and the time it actually took to complete the jobs. Is the report accurate? Did we capture the proper amounts of time charged, the right jobs, and the right standards for those jobs?" Jennifer looked at the report again and agreed that the accounting system had captured the activity of her group properly.

"But Jason," protested Jennifer, "we only did poorly on jobs 2003 and 3744. The rest of the jobs are in line with the standard. Those two jobs are ***impossible*** to complete in the standard time, fifty minutes each. Under ideal conditions, we will still spend three times as much labor on those jobs as called for in the standard. Every time we have to test similar products our labor performance goes right down the tubes. No one on my team is happy with this situation."

Jason needs help. The standard time Jason and Jennifer are referring to was developed by the engineering department and then placed into the cost system. The engineers estimated that the test for jobs 2003 and 3744 should take fifty minutes; actual tests are running around three hours. Jennifer contends that the standard is unfair. Obviously, something needs to happen here.

**Details**

Here is a sample report for Job 2003:

| *Operator* | *Job Number* | *Standard Time* | *Actual Time* | *Variance* | *Cost* |
|---|---|---|---|---|---|
| **Jen G.** | 2003 | 50 | 185 | (135) | ($1,620) |
| **Sean P.** | 2003 | 50 | 135 | (85) | ($1,020) |
| **Michele C.** | 2003 | 50 | 150 | (100) | ($1,200) |
| **Total** | | | 470 | (320) | ($3,840) |

**Assignments**

1) Provide Jason with an action plan to rectify the situation regarding the labor hours involved in the circuit board testing group. Include what may have to be done in order to achieve the standard time set forth by the engineering department. Consider how much involvement the engineering department, Jennifer and her team, and Jason should have in the final decision.

2) What would the financial implications of a standards change be for the company? What changes will the company see on (a) the labor performance report (example above), (b) the departmental budget report, and (c) the company monthly profit and loss statement?

a)

b)

c)

**Analysis**

3) Could a change in allocation methods change standard cost? What might be a fair way to allocate overhead costs to jobs 2003 and 3744?

4) The direct labor standard for the circuit board testing department is $12 per hour. The standard was developed based upon the average wage paid to the five department members in the department as of last December. Recently, two members have left for other departments and two new hires have joined. The new people earn $9.00 per hour each.

a) Should the standard cost for labor be changed? Why or why not?

b) How will your decision impact the department's monthly budget?

5) In a team meeting setting, discuss the impact for the following situation: In the process of revising the testing standard for Part 2003, the marketing team representative has indicated that the customer is extremely resistant to any price increases on the product. Additional costs of testing cannot be passed on to the customer. Hold a team brainstorming session to identify actions that could be taken to resolve the situation.

6) Use a job listing service such as www.monsterboard.com or www.hotjobs.com and look up a job description for a cost accountant or cost accounting manager. What are the specific job requirements?

___

___

___

___

___

___

___

___

### *Assignment 2-C: Case Study: The "Scrappers" Team*

Divisional manufacturing head Dennis Zimolic was pondering a problem. His Iowa manufacturing facility produced valves for the control of gas and oil through pipelines. Each valve needed to be machined from a rough casting to fit a specified tolerance. If the tested valve did not meet specs, the valve was sent to the weld shop for rework or scrapped. Valves that are declared scrap require all the material, labor, and overhead dollars charged to the valve to be written off to loss. Scrap losses had recently mounted to levels that exceeded the departmental budget and were starting to impact promised shipment dates to customers. Dennis knew it was time for action.

The standard cost system consisted of labor, material, and overhead, with overhead applied to the product based upon standard hours earned. Material standards were set by the purchasing department based upon historical costs for past orders of material and represent 60 percent of the product standard cost. A standard hour was earned every time a machine tool operator performed a labor operation that would take, on average, an hour to complete. The engineering department calculated averages after the completion of time-studied labor operations.

Dennis knew that his manufacturing supervisors and the machine tool operators did not have all the knowledge that they needed to significantly reduce scrap. They needed a team that included all the people that could have an effect on scrap. People from engineering, cost accounting, purchasing, scheduling, as well as machine operators and manufacturing supervisors, were called into a meeting. Dennis gave the team its charter. "Your team will be called the *scrappers*. It will be your job to look at every cause of scrap and make recommendations for changes that will result in higher levels of good product and lower scrap."

The new team was having its first meeting and already problems were evident. Nobody was willing to share information about the scrap problem for fear of making someone look bad. For example, the material for the valve was the responsibility of the purchasing department. If the material was found to be the source of the problem, the buyer from the purchasing department would look bad. Likewise, if a machine tool operation was found as a primary cause of scrap, then either operators were at fault or the engineers who designed the operation were wrong. Anyway the individual team members looked at the situation, they saw somebody taking the blame for what was going wrong.

**The Mechanics of Scrap**

In a typical manufacturing company, scrap results when something goes wrong in the transformation process. Scrap results when either the raw material used in the process fails or a machine or labor process fails to create an acceptable part. Line operators are normally responsible for ensuring that products produced will meet required specifications. When an operation fails to produce a good result, the standard costs from the current and previous operations charged to the part need to be written off to scrap expense.

The charge to scrap expense would include 100 percent of the material costs, the standard labor charge for all direct labor operations performed, and any overhead applied to the valve. If a part is scrapped when 50 percent of the standard labor has been performed, that would typically result in a scrap expense charge equal to 100 percent of the material, 50 percent of the standard labor, and 50 percent of the standard overhead. Parts scrapped closer to completion add more to the scrap expense than those scrapped early in the process.

**The Mechanics of Rework**

The manufacturing process begins when a large piece of metal, called a die-casting, arrives in the shop. The first operation inspects the casting for visible cracks. If the die-casting passes inspection, it is then sent to a machine tool that begins the process of shaving metal off the rough edges so the resulting valve can fit into a pipeline. If the operation takes off too much metal or a crack is discovered, a decision must be made to either scrap the die-casting or to rework the casting. If the rework option is chosen, the surface that has either a crack or has had too much material removed will be welded. The welding operation adds material that fills the crack or adds metal where needed. Once the rework is finished, the die-casting is placed back into normal operations. Once complete, the die-casting becomes a valve ready for duty in a pipeline.

**Assignments**

The *scrappers* team has been assigned the task of reducing scrap expense charges. The team will consist of a machine tool operator, an engineer, a purchasing agent, and a cost accountant. Use the following questions to guide the team to a successful resolution to the scrap problem.

1) How should the team go about resolving the issue of finding blame for the scrap problem?

2) What steps should the team take to understand the problem? What is the role of the management accountant in this process? What would you do if you were the purchasing department buyer?

3) What is Zimolic's role in the resolution of the scrap problem?

4) Assume you are appointed team leader for the *scrappers.* Develop a plan for what needs to be accomplished at the first meeting. Include team issues and technical issues.

5) Assume the role of an individual contributor on the *scrapper* team. What should you concentrate on during the initial meetings? Would this change if you were also a member of the engineering department?

________________________________________________

________________________________________________

________________________________________________

________________________________________________

________________________________________________

________________________________________________

________________________________________________

________________________________________________

________________________________________________

**Analysis**

Develop a report for Parts 23V891 and 47Y229 below. Determine if it is cost-justified to rework each valve. Use the following information:

| *Part Name* | *Standard Material* | *Standard Labor* | *Overhead* | *Rework Cost* | *Probability of Success** |
|---|---|---|---|---|---|
| **23V891 50%Fin** | $735.75 | $68.00 | $485.00 | $200.00 | 30% |
| **47Y229 75%Fin** | $900.00 | $75.00 | $535.00 | $300.00 | 50% |

*Note: If rework fails to make a good part, an additional rework charge will be required.

**Report**

Using the Internet, find information about how a total quality management (TQM) program could reduce scrap costs. A good source of information on TQM is located at http://deming.eng.clemson.edu/pub/den/files/ Prepare a slide presentation on the importance of total quality management. Be sure to include information on how a TQM program could be useful in reducing scrap. Your report should contain from 4 to 6 slides and be timed to last no more than 20 minutes.

### *Assignment 2-D: Case Study: The Vendor Blues*

Last year, Mario wanted to make a few extra dollars during the summer. Nearby was a golf course that did not have a sandwich shop. Mario decided to sell homemade sandwiches to golfers. After obtaining permission, Mario started selling sandwiches to golf league regulars playing in the early evening. He started with three varieties: ham, roast beef, and tuna fish. His main concern was how much to charge for his sandwiches. Could he sell enough on a given night to make his time worth while? Examining his costs, Mario found that sliced honey ham costs $3.99 per pound, roast beef costs $4.99 per pound, and tuna fish costs $2.50 per pound. A loaf of good rye or wheat bread costs $2.00 and yields 12 sandwiches. Mustard, mayo, and pickles cost $.15 per sandwich. Each sandwich would require a quarter pound of meat or tuna fish.

The missing part of the equation for Mario was the money he needs to make each night. Mario has the opportunity to make $7.00 per hour in wages at another job. Making the sandwiches, shopping for the food, delivering the product, and collecting the money take one hour for each task per day (four hours total).

1) What information needed to calculate standard costs is missing? Hint: How will you figure in the hour per day for shopping when costing out a ham sandwich?

______________________________________________

______________________________________________

______________________________________________

______________________________________________

______________________________________________

2) Assume that Mario wants to make at least $25 more per day than the $7.00 per hour he could earn elsewhere. His prices are $3.50 for tuna fish, $4.50 for ham, and $5.00 for roast beef. Each sandwich comes with a bag of chips that cost Mario $.25 that does not add money to the selling price of the sandwiches. Assuming no waste, how many sandwiches must he sell to reach his income goal if he sells an equal number of sandwiches?

______________________________________________

______________________________________________

______________________________________________

______________________________________________

3) How much money must Mario make each week to justify his sandwich business?

______________________________________________

______________________________________________

______________________________________________

______________________________________________

4) A new customer asks for a pastrami sandwich. What would be the job order cost for the special sandwich if the smallest amount of meat that could be purchased is one pound and the cost per pound is $5.99?

______________________________________________________________________

______________________________________________________________________

______________________________________________________________________

______________________________________________________________________

______________________________________________________________________

a) Should the extra meat purchased but not used be charged to the cost of the sandwich? Why or why not?

______________________________________________________________________

______________________________________________________________________

______________________________________________________________________

______________________________________________________________________

______________________________________________________________________

b) How should Mario's extra costs (shopping, making sandwiches, driving to the site) be charged to the sandwich?

______________________________________________________________________

______________________________________________________________________

______________________________________________________________________

______________________________________________________________________

______________________________________________________________________

______________________________________________________________________

______________________________________________________________________

# Chapter 3

## Activity-Based Costs

Traditional cost accounting systems assume that costs are the results of transforming products from raw material to finished goods. The transformation process takes materials and combines them in unique ways that make the outputs worth more than the sum of the inputs. For example, making a pizza includes combining many ingredients with various temperatures and time. If made correctly, the outcome is a delicious food treat that customers will pay for in amounts that more than compensate the maker for his/her costs. The good pizza maker transforms the dough, sauce, and toppings into a money-making product.

### *Assignment 3-A: Opening Story: Great Pizza*

Great pizza is transformed in the preparation activities and in the baker's oven. The function "cooking the pizza," for example, is so critical to the outcome of making pizza that without it pizza cannot be made. Traditional cost systems have looked to major transformation functions such as cooking the pizza to determine how costs are accumulated. Traditional systems would accumulate the cost of running and maintaining the oven, and the baker's time monitoring the process. The accumulated costs could then be divided over the oven baking times to determine allocated costs for the pizza.

For example, if a pepperoni pizza took 9 minutes to cook, overhead costs of $.78 could be allocated from the oven department's costs to each pizza made. See the chart below.

| | |
|---|---|
| Cooking time | 9 minutes |
| Total spending for oven | $7,750 per month |
| Estimated pizzas per month:<br>Capacity = 60 per hour<br>3 hours per day at peak<br>5 hours per day at ½ peak<br>30 days per month | 9,900 pizzas per month |
| Standard overhead per pizza, oven operation only | $0.78 per pizza* |

*This amount includes oven costs only; other overhead costs would have to be added for other operations such as preparation and delivery.

The traditional cost system generated an overhead charge of $.78 for each of the 9,900 pizzas made in a typical month. Upon closer examination of the activities involved in making the pizza, however, it was determined that variations existed in both the methods used to bake the pizza and the amount of baker's time required to monitor the process. Deep dish pizzas needed special handling and proper placement in the oven. Pizzas with "the works" required additional time. Special order pizzas required more time from the baker. The result of the study concluded that the overhead allocated to a normal, one-topping pizza was too high and the amount of overhead allocated to specials was too low.

1) What is the main difference between function-based costs and activity-based costs?

_______________________________________________

_______________________________________________

_______________________________________________

_______________________________________________

_______________________________________________

_______________________________________________

_______________________________________________

2) Could the use of activity-based costs improve the accuracy of the costs for a deep dish pizza? Explain.

_______________________________________________

_______________________________________________

_______________________________________________

_______________________________________________

_______________________________________________

3) Great Pizza is facing stiff competition from a local pizza chain. The selling price of a National Chain Pizza one-topping, 12-inch pizza is $1.50 less than Great Pizza's selling price. After visiting the store, you notice that National Chain Pizza has the same basic setup, oven, and toppings supplier that you have. What could this information possibly say about Great Pizza's function-based cost system?

_______________________________________________

_______________________________________________

_______________________________________________

_______________________________________________

_______________________________________________

_______________________________________________

_______________________________________________

The essence of activity-based costing is linking activities that drive costs to the products that should bear the burden for those activities. In the cases that follow, watch for opportunities to achieve more accurate costs by matching activity-driven costs to the products that cause those activities.

### *Assignment 3-B: Case Study: New England Wire*

Jack Tuthill, controller for New England Wire, a maker of hundreds of wire products, was visibly upset. Judy McCarthy from the sales department just mentioned in the company's monthly sales meeting that she believed the cost system was the cause of a decline in specialty wire sales. Jack couldn't believe his ears. How could the cost system be blamed for the sales department not doing their job? Jack and Judy agreed to meet after the meeting concluded.

Jack spoke first. "Judy, how could you possibly think that the cost system is to blame for your department's failure to hit last month's sales targets?" Judy was well prepared for Jack's question. "You see, Jack, Southern Wire has been underbidding us on specialty wire products at every opportunity. Most of the time they have bid a price that is below our cost system's standard cost. I can't compete with Southern on jobs where I can't even recover our costs with our sales price. I've also looked at Southern's latest financial statements and they are still making money. Something is very wrong here and I believe it's the cost system." Jack wouldn't budge. "Judy," Jack countered, "this cost system has been in place for over twenty years. We have never lost money before."

"Jack, listen," countered Judy. "the last time I visited our major customer, Northeastern Bell, the purchasing agent told me that the Southern salesperson was bragging about a new activity-based cost system that the company implemented six months ago. It seems that because of cost allocations, Southern had been routinely overcosting specialty wire products for years. The price cuts Southern offered Northeastern Bell were based upon a more accurate method of allocating costs. The purchasing agent asked me when were we going to wake up and lower our specialty prices."

1) What would you do if you were Jack? What are the typical symptoms of inaccurate costing? Discuss the implications to the company of Judy's allegations towards the cost system.

_______________________________________________________________________

_______________________________________________________________________

_______________________________________________________________________

_______________________________________________________________________

_______________________________________________________________________

_______________________________________________________________________

_______________________________________________________________________

2) Judy's comments imply that costs may have been overallocated to the specialty wire products. What steps must the company take to determine if this is true?

3) Assuming that a new cost system based upon allocating overhead according to activities is used, what is the likely outcome for the standard costs associated with specialty wire products? Will the costs go up or down? Explain.

4) What should happen to the standard cost of New England Wire's main product line, one inch copper wire, if the activity cost study indicates that the standard cost on the specialty product line should go down? Explain.

______________________________________________________________________

______________________________________________________________________

______________________________________________________________________

______________________________________________________________________

______________________________________________________________________

______________________________________________________________________

______________________________________________________________________

______________________________________________________________________

______________________________________________________________________

______________________________________________________________________

### *Assignment 3-C: Case Study: Big Board Games*

Big Board Games is a medium-sized toy company specializing in making the cardboard for popular board games. The product line consists of over 300 separate game boards, sold to over 100 companies worldwide. Each game comes with its own size and shape as well as colors and languages. Some games even include pop-up sections within the construction of the game boards.

Recently, the pop-up boards have experienced a large increase in sales. The sales department can sell all the pop-up boards manufacturing can make. Customers absorbed a 10 percent increase in prices for the product last month with no complaints. Field reports indicate that both major competitors of Big Board have recently dropped pop-up boards from their product lines.

The traditional standard cost system's product-line profitability report indicates that the pop-up board line is the best money maker in the company. Manufacturing, however, is not so sure. They report that pop-up boards are the most difficult board to manufacture and require constant attention by production workers and engineers. Vendors have a difficult time supplying materials that can be used for the pop-ups and maintenance is always repairing the manufacturing equipment used to make them. Scrap rates are also very high on this product line. Scheduling reports that on-time shipments of pop-up boards have been falling. Last month, only 85 percent of pop-up orders were on time, compared to 99 percent for all other product lines.

1) Does this company appear to be a candidate for activity-based costing? Why or why not?

2) Search the Internet for activity-based costing (ABC) accounting software using a major search engine such as AltaVista, Excite, Yahoo!, or Hotbot. From the top ten items returned, go to at least one vendor of ABC software. When you are at the Web site, find and report on at least two features of the software that might address the problems Big Board Games is currently having.

3) What steps should Big Board Games take to improve the profitability of the pop-up board line? How could these actions help pave the way for installing an activity-based cost system?

4) Assuming a new cost system is installed, what is most likely to happen to the product-line profitability report for the pop-up board line?

### *Assignment 3-D: Case Study: Thank You Cosmetics*

When companies adopt activity-based costing or activity-based management, one of the most common events that happen is a need for collecting information about activities.

Assume that you are assigned to the cost and activity collection team for Thank You Cosmetics, a manufacturer of pleasing cosmetics. Your job is to collect the activities of the shipping department for inclusion in an activity-based costing program.

As an observer of the department's activities, you have noted the following:

| Activity | Count/day | |
|---|---|---|
| Packing lipstick | 89 | 3 min per |
| Affixing special labels | 124 | 2 min per |
| Calling sales | 23 | 4 min per |
| Responding to customer inquiry | 34 | 6 min per |
| Packing mascara | 237 | 1 min per |
| Locating shipping materials | 31 | 8 min per |
| Entering cost data | 49 | 2 min per |
| Cleaning floor | 6 | 10 min per |
| Arranging for special freight | 14 | 12 min per |
| Meetings | 2 | 30 min per |

The following is known about the shipping department:

| | |
|---|---|
| Annual budget | $245,000 |
| Main products | Lipstick and mascara |
| Product variations | 49 lipsticks, 147 mascara shades |
| People in department | 6 employees, 1 supervisor |
| Sales cycle | 50% of business is from October to December, rest of business is evenly spread per month |

1) Develop a spreadsheet that takes the annual budget and spreads the dollars according to activities. Include a printout of your spreadsheet and a copy of your disk. In addition, describe the methodology you used to produce the spreadsheet.

2) Identify which activities are most likely value-added and which activities are non-value-added. Include reasons for your choices.

3) What could the company do to lower costs, given your answer to question 2?

# Chapter 4

## Cost-Profit-Volume

The issue of determining the break-even point for a business is critical to the understanding of how businesses actually work. Each month, a business faces certain costs of doing business that have very little to do with actual sales. These costs are fixed to the business, meaning they will occur each and every month. Fixed costs are incurred for things like property taxes, insurance, payback of loans, certain salaries, and more. These costs continue even if no sales take place and no customers are served.

Variable costs are the costs that are incurred each time a product is produced or a service given. They are required elements of the product or service. They include the material, labor, and overhead necessary to complete the transformation of materials into products for sale. With each additional product made, additional amounts of material, labor and overhead are combined into an item for sale.

Once made, individual product selling prices need to be high enough to cover the variable costs and leave some additional money left over to contribute to fixed costs. For example, let's assume that a regional potato chip maker, Crispy Chip, is selling an eight-ounce bag of chips for $.69 wholesale, which is the cost to the store. If Crispy Chip's variable costs for making the chips is $.39, a gross margin of $.30 per bag is obtained.

After the variable costs of making the chips are taken care of, Crispy Chip will have $.30 left over the help pay for the fixed costs of running the business. If enough bags of chips are sold, the business will make a profit. Calculating how many bags must be sold to cover both the variable and fixed costs of the business is called the break-even calculation.

### *Assignment 4-A: Opening Story: Fleet Skating Center*

The mayor of Providence, Rhode Island, Vincent A. "Buddy" Cianci, Jr., has reason to smile. His dream to bring more people to downtown Providence is working. Between the twice-a-month WaterFire that lights the river channel as it weaves its way through the city with torches, the new convention center, and the hit television show "Providence," there are now plenty of reasons for people to visit the city. Yet, in the winter months, the city seemed to lack a source of good, clean fun. Enter the Fleet Skating Center.

The Fleet Skating Center is an outdoor ice skating rink built in the heart of downtown Providence. Even though there are 14 indoor rinks within 30 miles of the city, the rink was an instant hit with the people. "In the first 16-week season of outdoor skating, the Center drew 82,500 skaters and grossed $550,000, leading city officials to predict that the rink will break even and perhaps turn a profit. Parks Superintendent Nancy Derrig said the revenues covered the rink's $100,000 debt service, the season's $15,000 administrative fee paid to a company managing the rink, and the rink's unspecified operating expenses."[1]

Critics of the skating center, although impressed with the revenue and attendance in the first season, expressed some concern for the long term. If the Fleet Skating Center was not profitable, the city of Providence might have to make up the operating losses.

1) How would knowing the break-even point for the skating rink help Parks Superintendent Derrig keep the critics quite?

2) Assuming all known costs are listed above and each skater of the rink paid an equal admission price, how much could the variable costs per skater be if the rink were to achieve breakeven?

[1] *It's Time for Skating* sans *Ice*, Jonathan D. Rockoff, *Sunday Providence Journal*, April 4, 1999, p. B1.

3) The Fleet Skating Center is shut down every year around April 15. The rink could then be used for an inline skating rink, street hockey, dances, or any other use the officials might come up with. Assuming they use the rink for the production of additional revenue, which variable costs change and why? What costs would remain fixed?

4) Fixed costs remain fixed if they operate within a relevant range. What costs would be relevant to the continued running of the rink as an inline skating park?

5) Assuming the Fleet Skating Center has a liability insurance policy costing $50,000 for the ice skating season and would have to purchase an additional policy for inline skating amounting to $300,000, is this cost a fixed or a variable cost? Explain your answer.

## *Assignment 4-B: Case Study: Where the Rubber Meets the Plastic*

The dream of a new company called Greenman Technologies, Inc., back in 1995 was to take used automobile tires, break them down, and combine the resulting material with plastic into usable products for sale. The products would have a very high content of recyclable materials obtained at low costs. Manufacturing would convert the used tires and plastics into usable consumer products such as trash cans and storage bins. In order to make money on this business idea, the company needed to obtain used tires and recycled plastics at the lowest possible cost, convert them into products, and then sell them for a profit.

The company discovered that obtaining used tires was not a problem, although the cost to pick up and deliver them to its manufacturing facilities was higher than anticipated. Additionally, the manufacturing process of combining the rubber with the plastic proved to be challenging. Lastly, the company found that the market for trash cans and storage bins put them in direct competition with well-established companies. All of these facts put pressure on the company's ability to make money.

**Project Details**

The company president has asked your team to perform a break-even analysis on the business in light of the following facts:

- Used tires cost $2.50 each to buy and transport to the manufacturing facility.
- Plastic bottles used in the process cost $2 per pound of ground materials when delivered.
- Both products contain 50 percent tires and 50 percent plastics.
- Manufacturing processes add $3 per trash can and $4 per storage bin to the process.
- Fixed costs per month are $570,000; general and administrative costs are $280,000 fixed plus $.50 per sale item variable.
- Selling price of the trash can is $8 and the storage container is $9.
- Projected volume is expected to be 60 percent trash cans and 40 percent storage containers.

1) Prepare a break-even analysis for Greenman Technologies for the trash can and storage bin business. At what volume of sales will the company break even?

2) What would be the new break even if the fixed costs were reduced by $200,000 per month?

3) Visit Environmental Rubber of Puerto Rico at http://www.eppr.com/ERPR/ Find out how the process of turning used tires into usable products works. Prepare a report to management that summarizes your findings, especially as it pertains to areas where Greenman Technologies could reduce their present costs.

4) Use a multiple search engine such as http://www.google.com to find other firms in the USA that are converting rubber into useful products. Search on key words such as "recycled tires." Write about what these companies are doing that might help Greenman Technologies management control or reduce costs.

### *Assignment 4-C: Case Study: CommonPlaces Aims to Bring College Students into a Common Net Space*

CommonPlaces LLC is a new company working to corner the college student market. Their goal is to tap the college market. They realized that the college market was underserved by the Internet and it was time to do something to crack the market. CommonPlaces has completed interviews with more than 2,000 college students, formed alliances with 253 colleges, baited national advertisers, and announced the beta launch of its new site, CollegeBytes.com. The site will feature course descriptions, campus and off-campus events, and links to student groups.

**Project Details**

CommonPlaces plans on making money with revenue generated through advertising sales. The advertising sales must exceed costs such as how much it will cost to update the site, cost of the server, cost of software, staff salary, monthly Internet connection, and monthly rental cost of a T-1 line.

**The Process**

CommonPlaces developed a college portal with personalized functions and a way for groups to develop their own sites to give students tools to communicate with each other online. In order to accomplish this CommonPlaces must have a lot of knowledge of the Internet business. The employees' salaries at CommonPlaces cost $23,000 a month. Other costs include $5,200 per month for the building rental, $500 per month for electricity, $400 for the monthly Internet connection, and $1,200 for the monthly rental of the T-1 line. Each ad sold costs CommonPlaces a one-time charge of $5,000 to produce and place it on the Web site.

The sales process is based on the number of impressions an ad gets per month. For example, each unique time an ad is viewed is considered an impression, so if the Web page that your ad is on is viewed 100,000 times and you paid for only 100,000 impressions, then your ad has fulfilled your request and is taken off that page. You pay a certain amount for the number of impressions you order.

**The Project**

CommonPlaces charges a certain amount per guaranteed ad view impression during a one-month period. Their prices are $2,500 per 100,000 impressions per month and $6,000 per 250,000 impressions per month. The ad is kept on the desired page for as long as it takes until it has seen the number of impressions requested.

**The Task**

Determine how many additional contracts for 250,000 impressions at $6,000 per contract CommonPlaces needs on their new site in order to break even, given that they have sold 15 contracts for 100,000 impressions per month at $2,500 each.

Advertising prices found at http://www.gamehub.net/advert.htm

## *Assignment 4-D: Case Study: FinancialNet.Com*

FinancialNet.com (or FN.com) is a full service online financial service company. Borne on the Internet, FN.com is a business that seeks customers of all backgrounds and income for purchasing various financial services. The first product for sale on the Internet site was term life insurance. Next, the company added home owners and auto insurance sold to residents of states where state law permitted.

The company recruited agents that would act as online assistants for handling the individual needs of potential and existing clients. The online agents entered into live chat windows with customers, providing them with immediate answers to their questions. This proved very popular with customers and the business grew rapidly.

The company was breaking new ground. On the good side, the agency was selling products at a very fast rate. On the bad side, however, sales were expanding faster than the company's ability to hire and train new online agents. Customers were beginning to ask for products not yet offered for sale. New competition was entering the online marketplace every week.

**Project Details**

The president of the company has asked you or your team to prepare a proposal for entering into the financial planning business. The new online product is estate planning. Included in your proposal must be a break-even analysis for entering into this business.

Estate planning advisory services are charged on a set fee basis: $3,000 for basic planning packages and $8,000 for estate planning including the establishment of trusts.

Fixed costs include an office charge of $48,000 per month, computer lease expense of $800 per month for six computer stations and a dedicated server, salaries and wages of $25,000 per month, and insurance costs of $350 per month. In addition, Internet connection and Web page housing will cost $1,750 per month and training costs are budgeted at $1,500 per month. Variable costs include a 15 percent sales commission on the product's profit margin to all new customer sales 5 percent on profit margin for repeat sales.

**The Tasks**

1) Determine break even for the new business assuming the company anticipates 60 percent of sales to be estate plans including trusts and 40 percent of sales will be basic planning packages.

2) Does the number sound reasonable, given the fact that the company is planning on hiring six professional online agents to work exclusively on the new products? Why or why not?

## *Assignment 4-E: Case Study: Communication Counts*

A major part of a person's success as a managerial accountant can come from the ability to clearly present information in the form of graphs and charts. Monthly meetings, department gatherings, and even Web-based reports are calling for visual interpretation. The following exercises will give direction and challenge in compiling accounting information through the use of charts and graphs.

**Keep It Simple**

The KIS principle, keep it simple, is always a good idea. Presentations at monthly meetings are not the place to present complex technical ideas and concepts. A short, simple message will go a long way in both communicating the information you want to give and in having your audience actually get your message.

**Chart Tips**

Microsoft PowerPoint charts are a quick and easy way of putting a presentation together. However, you will need to be careful not to pack too much information into any given slide. The purpose of showing a slide during a presentation is to reinforce a concept being presented, not to make a point. The slide gives you backup to your central message, but the spoken message is the presentation. Inexperienced speakers often attempt to let the slides take over the presentation for them. When you create your slides, use short phrases and key words that will trigger your main ideas.

1) Create a presentation for a monthly cost control meeting given the following:

Material budget: $4.00/unit; actual $4.01
Material usage: 200 units actual, 210 units standard

What will be the central point of your presentation? Write a note in bullet form listing the major points you will make about your presentation.

2) Prepare and present a short informational report on the importance of knowing what a business's break-even point is. Remember to keep the information on the slide to a minimum. The report should include your rough outline and your slide presentation.

3) Refer to the information in the Fleet Skating Center opening case (Assignment 4-A). Prepare a slide presentation to the management of the center detailing the present profit picture of the rink. Also prepare information about the possible revenue and profit potential for using the rink in a 28-week session for inline skating.

# Chapter 5

## Responsibility Accounting

### *Assignment 5-A: Opening Story: Where's the Beef?*

Beef's Best, a fast-food chain featuring great roast beef sandwiches and flame-grilled hamburgers, recently hired Devin Chaput as their new store manager for the Portland location. Devin has worked his way up the management ladder, performing virtually all of the jobs necessary to run a Beef's Best store. Devin really wants to impress his boss, Connie Schmidt, the regional manager.

Back at the regional office, Connie has been looking over the numbers from the stores reporting to her. Sales are up about 5 percent overall compared to the similar quarter last year, but only a few stores are reporting profit gains. Devin's store is not one of the stores reporting profit gains. Connie has tremendous confidence in Devin's ability to run the Portland store, but looking at the numbers she is starting to have some doubts.

Devin knows the Portland store sales are up only 3 percent and that profits are off. Beef costs, negotiated by regional purchasing, have been increasing at rates above forecasted levels. Other things, however, are actually going right. The store is cleaner then it has been in years, and staff turnover as measured by the number of people needed to replace workers who leave or are fired has been cut in half. A regional quality inspector for food and customer service gave Devin's store its highest rating. Controllable costs were in line with profit targets. In addition, last month the business was publicly awarded by the local chamber of commerce for an innovative training program that is helping previously unemployable people get jobs.

Still, Devin was worried about how Connie would react to the profit picture for the Portland store. Devin's store bonus is tied directly to store profitability. With the current profit results slipping below last year's profit figures, Devin will not receive a bonus.

1) What are the components of a good performance measurement system?

______________________________________________________________________

______________________________________________________________________

______________________________________________________________________

______________________________________________________________________

______________________________________________________________________

______________________________________________________________________

2) How should Devin's performance as manager of the Portland store be measured?

3) What role should nonfinancial measurements have in measuring the performance of a store like Beef's Best? Why are they important?

4) What steps could Devin take to improve his store's financial performance?

5) What dangers are present if Devin takes as many steps as possible to improve the store's profits? Could any of these actions cause long-term problems?

## *Responsibility Accounting*

The goal of for-profit companies is to maximize the wealth of its owners, the shareholders. This is accomplished when the collective decisions and actions of all employees result in profitable business transactions. To help ensure that employees are acting in ways that will lead to increased shareholder wealth, companies employ a managerial control system. A responsibility accounting system works within a managerial control system to provide a structure for controlling activities and evaluating performance. In other words, responsibility accounting attempts to get everybody in the company making decisions and taking actions that will result in the best interests of the shareholders.

Sometimes, however, a conflict results between the goals and objectives of the company and the goals and objectives of individuals. Individuals could make decisions that make them look good and produce short-term gains at the expense of the long-term goals of the company. The following case studies will focus on how the conflicts between individual goals and company goals can be resolved within a responsibility accounting system.

## *Assignment 5-B: Case Study: Hamilton Standard, Farmington Division*

Tony Rice once said, "They will never fire me for having too much inventory, but there will be hell to pay if I run out." Tony was the former material manager of the Hamilton Standard, Farmington Division plant. For several years, Tony made sure that the Farmington plant always had enough parts to assemble and test the computers produced by manufacturing.

The performance of the plant was measured in two ways. First, monthly sales targets were established for dollar volumes and on-time shipments. Second, the plant had profit targets to meet. As long as enough products were shipped on time and the plant ran within profit targets, management's performance was given a good rating. Annual bonuses for senior management were awarded for meeting or exceeding targets.

Tony Rice was promoted to plant manager of Farmington in the mid-1990s. Performance measurement of the Farmington plant by Hamilton Standard soon changed. Customers began to demand products with lower costs and higher quality. Overhead costs needed to be significantly reduced. Parts inventory became a target for reduction. The old way of simply buying more parts to ensure shipment performance just wouldn't work anymore.

New emphasis was placed on receiving higher levels of quality parts from vendors, cutting down on all nonvalue-added costs, reducing overhead, and increasing the number of computers manufacturing could make in a given shift. Spending on rework,* which is the money spent to bring a computer that had failed an in-line quality test back up to quality specifications, needed to be drastically cut. All of the above actions were new to

Mr. Rice and the other members of plant management.

*Rework in the Farmington plant happened whenever a computer failed an inline quality test. Instead of scrapping the computer, the individual components of the system were evaluated separately. When the defective component part was discovered, the part would be replaced and a new round of testing began. Once the repaired computer passed the test it originally failed, the computer was put back in the production line. All work associated with this activity was called rework.

1) Develop a new performance measurement system for the Farmington plant. Be sure to include quality, cost reduction, and inventory levels in addition to the traditional measurements of sales and profits.

2) What are the major performance challenges facing the senior management team at Farmington? How will the system developed above address the major performance challenges?

3) Tony Rice and his management team have a profit goal to meet each month. How could the profit goal possibly cause conflict with other goals of the division? For example, how could a high profit target cause inventory to increase to unacceptably high levels?

4) How could lower rework levels help the Farmington plant meet all divisional performance goals?

5) Carrying lower quantities of required parts will reduce inventory levels. When companies reduce inventory levels, what must happen to the quality of the parts they carry and why?

6) Provide a list of possible nonfinancial measurements that the Farmington plant should consider adding to their performance measurement system.

7) Mr. Rice is looking at an offer from a vendor who offers to carry a 10-day supply of a critical, high-usage part if Tony is willing to spend an additional $1 per part. They would deliver all needed parts via overnight shipment on a daily basis, eliminating the need for the plant to carry inventory. Under what circumstances would this offer be attractive to Mr. Rice?

## *Assignment 5-C: Case Study: GreenWoman's Acquisition*

**Background**

GreenWoman Industries, Inc., a company that aims to be the nation's largest recycler of used automobile tires, recently acquired a small tire recycler, Second Spin, Inc., which is located in Missouri. The former owner of Second Spin, Peter Dewitt, must now report his performance to GreenWoman's headquarters. GreenWoman (GW) organizes its divisions as investment centers with the divisional managers responsible for sales, profits, and return on investment. Dewitt and his management team are given plenty of leeway in making decisions about running the business. In return for the high degree of autonomy, GW expects full reporting and accountability.

Dewitt and his management team are facing the first review of performance under the new company. Jackie Simian, the cost accounting manager, has just looked over a memo received from GW's corporate finance department. Jackie says, "Peter, what is this $84,500 charge from GW for allocated services all about? That amount totally wiped out our net profit for the month. I thought we were running this business as an independent division. What could the people at GW possibly be doing for us to justify this outrageous charge?" Peter responded, "Look, Jackie, I'm not really sure how the corporate charge got so high but I do remember the GW folks say that we would have to cover some expenses. Why don't you give them a call and get some details?"

After calling GW headquarters, Jackie found out that the corporate allocated charge was based upon the prior month's sales and was meant to cover the costs of running the headquarters. If Second Spin continued to increase sales each month, the headquarters charge would continue to rise. Peter was beside himself. "How are we ever going to show a profit in this business if the headquarters charge keeps growing directly with sales? Don't those GW people have a clue?" The situation was beginning to frustrate Peter. For the second month in a row, Second Spin failed to hit profit targets by an amount very close to the corporate charge.

1) Comment on the fairness of GreenWoman's method of allocating costs to Second Spin.

______________________________________________________________________

______________________________________________________________________

______________________________________________________________________

______________________________________________________________________

______________________________________________________________________

______________________________________________________________________

2) Does the present allocation system create goal congruence for the Second Spin management team? Why or why not?

3) If the present system of charging divisional overhead is left unchanged, what do you predict that Peter and his team will most likely do? Why?

4) As a member of the GreenWoman divisional management team, what changes could you suggest that might help Peter Dewitt and his team? Note: Decreasing the charge from the division is not an option.

### *Assignment 5-D: Case Study: Whitman Industries Performance Measurement*

The engineering standards department was working late again tonight. Sam, the industrial engineer, had just finished inputting new labor and material standards on one hundred separate parts. Having accurate prices on each part was critical to the development of the new budget for the Rochester division. Additional work on the budget had to wait for Sam's input.

The cost accounting manager, Cindy, was also working late. Unfortunately, her work had ground to a halt until Sam could finish his work. Cindy decided to ask Sam what was taking him so long. "Sam, how's the job going? When will you finish?" Sam replied, "Cindy, this is taking me longer than I thought. Did you know that Hawkins (the purchasing manager) has been all over my case about not changing several of the standards until next year? He says that the standards changes I am making will cause his year-end material spending variance report to look bad and he will miss his bonus. Can you imagine?" "Sam," Cindy replied, "you know you have my full backing for all changes to the standards. After all, you have the proper documentation for the standard change, and the accuracy of the cost system is more important than Hawkins' bonus." "Try telling that to Hawkins," replied Sam.

Here are the most recent changes to the standard material prices:

| Part Description | Present Standard | New Standard | Standard Change | Dollar Impact |
|---|---|---|---|---|
| Flux Capacitor | $.00234 | $.00230 | ($.00004) | ($23,000) |
| Widget Bakelite | $1.245 | $1.347 | $.1020 | ($34,500) |
| Lamar DipSwitch | $534 | $541 | $7.00 | ($123,000) |
| Whip Winger | $34 | $32 | ($2.00) | $14,700 |

1) What are the potential ethical problems presented in the facts above? Be sure to speak from both Sam's and Cindy's point of view.

2) Comment on the managerial performance report for the purchasing manager. Is Whitman Industries measuring the right thing? Why or why not?

3) The next day, Hawkins comes to Cindy's office and requests her help in explaining the $123,000 variance on the Lamar DipSwitch part. What additional information do you need to help Hawkins make a case for the rising material standard cost?

### *Assignment 5-E: Case Study: Kitten Care, LLC*

Kitten Care, LLC, is a long-term care facility specializing in providing extended care to animals, especially cats. The business was borne when Miss Kitty, a beloved pet of a multimillionaire, was bequeathed a lifetime of pampering. In the last will and testament of her former owner, Miss Kitty was given an endowment to continue her former lifestyle until her death. Miss Kitty always had plenty of other animals around her, so when the former New Castle estate was converted for her use, accommodations for another 30 or so pets were included in the renovations. The will also stated that any property built or modified for use by Miss Kitty should continue to be a sanctuary for animals. When Miss Kitty passed away, Kitten Care, LLC, was established.

Currrent owners Lucy and Paul Jones have established a profitable business taking care of pampered pets of the rich and famous. Services include boarding pets for weeks at a time, weekend getaways, and the Miss Kitty adoption service for pets whose owners have passed away. Lucy and Paul have run their business on three basic strategies. First, give the pets uncompromising service. Second, treat the customers with dignity and respect. Third, maintain a continuously improving business that increases profits each year.

As devoted pet lovers, Lucy and Paul find the first strategy comes naturally. Pets trusted to their care receive uncompromising care for all their needs. Kitten Care, LLC, employs a veterinarian, a pet nutritionist, a pet groomer, and several support personnel for cleaning and pet exercising. In addition, they spend $10,000 per year to repair furniture, replace rugs, and to repair other minor items as needed.

The second strategy consists of treating the customers exceptionally well. To accomplish this goal, new services have been introduced, such as daily e-mail updates on pet health, certificates of good behavior, listings of all food eaten, details of dog walks, and free grooming. Bills detail every charge with clarity.

The third strategy is to continuously improve both the quality of the pet care and the profitability of the business. Lucy and Paul made some improvements over the last two years, but the pace and frequency of the improvements have slowed considerably. Last year, for example, Lucy and Paul needed to reach into the Miss Kitty endowment for $7,000 to cover a shortfall in their improvement fund.

**Team Assignment**

1) Meet with your team. Refer to the list of suggested team duties and responsibilities in Appendix A. Using the list as a starting point, prepare a list of the individual team members' responsibilities that your team will use to use to complete this assignment.

_______________________________________________

_______________________________________________

_______________________________________________

_______________________________________________

_______________________________________________

_______________________________________________

_______________________________________________

_______________________________________________

_______________________________________________

2) Focusing on the team, prepare a second list of responsibilities for the entire team. Be sure to get each team member to agree to the items that appear on your list.

3) Compare lists from items 1 and 2 and explain any differences. What is different about a class project group and a work team?

4) Visit http://www.workteams.unt.edu/proceed/porter.htm and read the article "Are we teaching people not to work in teams: Reflections on team based assignments in the college classroom," by Gayle Porter. In your experience, what are the elements of good teamwork on team-based assignments?

**Assignment (Teams and Individuals)**

5) Judy and Paul have asked you (your team) to help begin an activity-based responsibility accounting system. Develop a list of activities that drive costs within Kitten Care. List the costs into value-added and nonvalue-added activities.

6) The balanced scorecard has four perspectives: financial, customer, process and learning, and growth. Describe how a balanced scorecard approach to Kitten Care, LLC, might be use. Be sure to address all four perspectives in your answer.

7) Judy and Paul would like to reduce costs while making continuous improvements to their business. Explain how Kitten Care, LLC, might approach the task of developing activities and activity drivers to help measure continuous improvement. Be sure to focus first on which activity driver is appropriate for each identified activity.

8) Kitten Care, LLC, has identified four major internal processes. They are feeding the animals, exercising animals, caring for customers, and cleaning the facility. How would you or your team decide which activities within the internal processes are targets for cost reduction? Identify a possible cost reduction for each internal process.

## *Assignment 5-F: Case Study: True Tested Company*

### Monthly Update Meeting

One of the biggest challenges facing a new management accountant is preparing for the monthly update meeting. The monthly update meeting is the opportunity to compare actual results to budget and to explain why the numbers are different. The meeting brings together the people who were responsible for creating the actual numbers with the people they report to. If the results are good, the meeting can be very informative and pleasant. If the numbers indicate problems, the meeting can get interesting.

The management accountant needs to be extremely careful when putting together the numbers for a monthly update meeting. First of all, the numbers must be right. If even a small mistake enters a graph presented to upper management, large amounts of creditability can be lost. Also, the accountant should prepare answers to any and all questions the data is likely to suggest. Having a solid knowledge of where each number came from is essential to answering questions correctly.

The presentation format for the meeting is typically charts projected on a large screen. Handouts of the charts should be prepared and passed out before the meeting starts to all meeting participants. A rehearsed "script" or story line for each chart should be reviewed for clarity and accuracy. Charts should be simple, clear, and carry only high-level summary information.

**Exercises**

For the following questions, use the following data for True tested Company, Inc.

| **For the Month of May** | **Budget** | **Actual** |
|---|---|---|
| Sales | $450,000 | $420,000 |
| Cost of Sales | $325,000 | $330,000 |
| General & Administrative | $58,000 | $57,000 |
| Net Income | $20,000 | $18,500 |
| Customer Returns | 14 | 12 |
| On-time shipments (%) | 97% | 92% |
| Quality expenses | $150,000 | $165,000 |
| Personnel Department | $13,000 | $12,000 |
| Finance Department | $20,000 | $18,000 |
| Corporate Charges | $47,000 | $52,000 |

1) Prepare a sales performance chart for the month comparing budget to actual. Add a few keywords that will help explain why the current activity missed the target. Create a rough drawing of the proposed chart.

2) Prepare a cost of sales performance chart. Add explanations for missing budget.

Notes to accompany presentation.

3) Quality expenses were over budget by $15,000. This was due to a new quality program aimed at preventing defects. The positive effects of the program will not be reflected in the numbers until many months in the future. Prepare a chart that highlights the "good news" on quality.

4) Visit http://www.qualitymag.com/articles/dec98/1298cs.html and look at the featured tool shop monitoring system. Assuming this tool shop is a part of the above company, develop a chart that highlights the recent tool shop activities.

5) Using the above information, prepare a 15-minute group presentation using slide preparation software such as Microsoft PowerPoint. Be sure to include brief explanations for your numbers.

# Chapter 6

## Operational Budgets

Planning and control are often linked to success within organizations. Planning looks ahead to predict the direction of the company. Control helps a company keep on track with the plan. The formal budgeting system is an important part of ensuring that the plans established by the company will be met.

Budgeting requires the establishment of plans for both revenues and expenses. Each major element of the plan should be identified in both time and amount. For example, a budgeting system should identify the sales items in quantity and the time period when the items will be sold. Expenses that are required to support budgeted levels of sales should be added.

The following cases will explore budgeting from a functional and an activity-based budgeting system.

### *Assignment 6-A: Opening Story: Connect Circuit Boards*

Connect Circuit Board, Inc. (CCB), is preparing the budget process for the year 2001. The president of CCB has issued the following statement:

"The year 2001 will be a landmark year for CCB. We are looking for growth of 20 percent in sales and 20 percent in earnings, fueled by continued expansion in international markets and healthy growth domestically. Our profit targets are ambitious* and will require vision, skill, and, in some cases, sacrifice. As we proceed into the budget process, please create the most realistic budget information possible. The executive team must know today where our profit challenges for the year 2001 will be. Realistic numbers will eliminate unnecessary surprises. Budget review will begin with the distribution center budget on the 15 of next month."

Your team is to assemble the proposed budget for the year 2001 for the distribution center. Actual spending for the first nine months of 2000 is presented on the next page.

*Profit for 2000 is projected to be in a range from 16 to 18 percent.

## *Distribution Department Budget/Actual Report*

| | September 2000 | | | Nine Months Ending September 2000 | | |
|---|---|---|---|---|---|---|
| | ***Actual*** | ***Budget*** | ***Variance*** | ***Actual*** | ***Budget*** | ***Variance*** |
| **Wages** | 47,053.00 | 49,130.00 | 2,077.00 | 421,200.00 | 442,170.00 | 20,970.00 |
| **Fringe Benefits** | 13,645.00 | 14,739.00 | 1,094.00 | 124,250.00 | 132,651.00 | 8,401.00 |
| **Headcount** | 15.00 | 16.00 | 1.00 | 15.00 | 16.00 | 1.00 |
| **Supplies** | 3,563.00 | 3,200.00 | (363.00) | 38,233.00 | 28,800.00 | (9,433.00) |
| **Maintenance** | 7,869.00 | 6,000.00 | (1,869.00) | 60,230.00 | 54,000.00 | (6,230.00) |
| **Computers** | 1,485.00 | 1,000.00 | (485.00) | 13,900.00 | 9,000.00 | (4,900.00) |
| **Freight—Overnight** | 5,200.00 | 5,500.00 | 300.00 | 56,800.00 | 49,500.00 | (7,300.00) |
| **Freight—Surface** | 12,400.00 | 6,800.00 | (5,600.00) | 99,350.00 | 61,200.00 | (38,150.00) |
| **Warehouse** | 23,800.00 | 22,000.00 | (1,800.00) | 214,300.00 | 198,000.00 | (16,300.00) |
| **Insurance** | 5,000.00 | 5,000.00 | -- | 45,000.00 | 45,000.00 | -- |
| **Property taxes** | 7,500.00 | 7,300.00 | (200.00) | 67,500.00 | 65,700.00 | (1,800.00) |
| ***Totals*** | **127,515.00** | **120,669.00** | **(6,846.00)** | **1,140,763.00** | **1,086,021.00** | **(54,742.00)** |

1) Prepare an estimate of fourth quarter actual spending. Be sure to take into consideration the spending in the month of September. Enter your answer on the chart.

***Distribution Department Budget/Actual Report***

Nine Months Ending September 2000

| | Actual | Budget | Variance | Oct | Nov | Dec | Total 2000 |
|---|---|---|---|---|---|---|---|
| **Wages** | 421,200.00 | 442,170.00 | 20,970.00 | | | | |
| **Fringe Benefits** | 124,250.00 | 132,651.00 | 8,401.00 | | | | |
| **Headcount** | 15.00 | 16.00 | 1.00 | | | | |
| **Supplies** | 38,233.00 | 28,800.00 | (9,433.00) | | | | |
| **Maintenance** | 60,230.00 | 54,000.00 | (6,230.00) | | | | |
| **Computers** | 13,900.00 | 9,000.00 | (4,900.00) | | | | |
| **Freight—Overnight** | 56,800.00 | 49,500.00 | (7,300.00) | | | | |
| **Freight—Surface** | 99,350.00 | 61,200.00 | (38,150.00) | | | | |
| **Warehouse** | 214,300.00 | 198,000.00 | (16,300.00) | | | | |
| **Insurance** | 45,000.00 | 45,000.00 | -- | | | | |
| **Property Taxes** | 67,500.00 | 65,700.00 | (1,800.00) | | | | |
| ***Totals*** | 1,140,763.00 | 1,086,021.00 | (54,742.00) | | | | |

2) Use the estimate calculated in question 1 to create an estimate of the full year 2000 spending. Enter your answer on the chart.

3) On a separate piece of paper, prepare a full year 2001 budget, based upon actual spending and the president's sales and profit goals.

4) Prepare a presentation for the budget review team. Include financial schedules for the years 2000 and 2001. Document important assumptions used in calculating your numbers. Be prepared to defend your budget, especially as it contributes to the president's target of 20 percent profit for the year 2000.

5) The actual spending for 2000 is 5 percent over budget through the third quarter of the year 2000. Fourth quarter spending plans need to include a spending reduction from the distribution center to meet year 2000 financial goals. The spending reduction

needs to be explained. Where will the savings come from and how will it be achieved? This question will come up in the president's review meeting.

________________________________________

________________________________________

________________________________________

________________________________________

________________________________________

________________________________________

________________________________________

________________________________________

### *Assignment 6-B: Case Study: Sam's Snow Job*

As a young intern for Continental Can Corporation, Terry was enjoying her rotation through the accounting department's various functions. During her stay, Terry was exposed to the company's budget cycle. The budget consisted of the corporate office establishing a profit target and strategic direction, followed by a formal review of all sales and expenses proposed to meet the targets. Allen Robbe was the budget manager. Allen had several years' experience and was eager to share his knowledge with Terry.

"Terry, I would like you to handle the maintenance accounts in this year's budget," Allen said. "Take a good look at the spending we have experienced over the last two years and project that information into a proposed spending plan for next year. Please be sure to use an amount that will cover snow removal expenses if we get hit hard this winter. I don't want a repeat of the problem we ran into in 1998."

Terry began her budget preparation by looking at all the invoices that were charged to the snow removal account in 1998. Terry discovered several charges for a service called Sam's Snow Job, a local snow removal company. Sam's Snow Job was called into action on three occasions to remove snow in excess of a foot from the employee parking lot and to clean snow and ice from the sidewalks around the building. The 1998 charges amounted to $20,000 against a budget of zero. 1999 and 2000 actual expenditures for snow removal were zero. Terry knew she would have to talk fast to get any new budget dollars for Sam's Snow Job.

1) Assuming you are Terry, what evidence could you present during the budget review to support a claim for $20,000 for snow removal?

2) Consider that the national weather service forecasts a mild winter with only one or two storms likely that would require the services of Sam's Snow Job. How should this information be used in the budget process?

3) Allen Robbe has asked for a budget walk-through prior to the actual budget meeting. In preparation for this meeting, prepare a slide and an explanation for the snow removal budget.

### *Assignment 6-C: Case Study: Universal Learning Systems*

Universal Learning Systems, or ULS, is a company on a fast track. Selling systems that help companies learn, grow, and collaborate has become very popular. The service requires trained instructors to work with teams from companies. Sales are expanding faster than the company can hire qualified instructors.

The lead time to train a qualified instructor is six weeks. In that time, ULS must spend $3,500 per week per instructor for wages and certification fees. Each qualified instructor can produce billings of $150 per hour, or $6,000 per week. Additional fixed business costs include $75,000 per month.

The chief executive officer of ULS, Cal Valatore, has asked your team to put together a training budget for the next six months with the following objectives in mind. First, the training budget cannot exceed 50 percent of current sales revenue. Second, recruiting expenses, not including training, cannot exceed $1,500 per person. Currently, ULS has 20 trained instructors, each billing 35 hours per week.

1) Prepare a training budget for ULS that hires as many people as possible and still meets the objectives specified by the chief executive officer. Assume that the maximum number of individuals that can be started in any given week is six and that newly trained people will immediately begin to bill $6,000 per week once fully trained.

2) How many people can the company hire at the beginning of the seventh month?

3) After six months, the company discovers a way to train 12 new hires per week. Does the company have enough revenue to support the training and still meet the chief executive officer's objectives? Don't forget to add in the $1,500 hiring costs per person.

________________________________________________________________________

________________________________________________________________________

________________________________________________________________________

________________________________________________________________________

________________________________________________________________________

________________________________________________________________________

________________________________________________________________________

________________________________________________________________________

## *Assignment 6-D: Case Study: Rochester Seal Company*

Rochester Seal Company (RCS) sells products that make a door or window seal itself from outside elements. Selling everything from rubber lining to metal insulated plates, the Rochester Seal Company ships its products to the housing and automotive industry. Each year, the budget cycle begins in the same place: the sales forecast.

### Rochester Seal Company
### Sales Forecast in Dollars

| | Actual 2001 | Budget 2002 |
|---|---|---|
| **Housing** | | |
| Window seals | $ 457,888 | $ 600,000 |
| Door seals | 2,353,433 | 2,450,000 |
| Insulating kits | 204,590 | 300,000 |
| **Subtotals** | $3,015,911 | $3,350,000 |
| **Automotive** | | |
| Ford | $ 3,434,904 | $ 3,300,000 |
| GM | 4,545,454 | 4,800,000 |
| Toyota | 2,749,491 | 3,000,000 |
| Honda | 300,056 | 750,000 |
| **Subtotals** | $11,029,905 | $11,850,000 |
| **Total** | **$14,045,816** | **$15,200,000** |

**Emphasis areas for 2002:**

a. Sales increase of 8.2%
b. Reduction in costs of 10%
c. Expansion of product line in automotive
d. Finish budget by Dec. 31

**Part A**

Part #47H59830-3 is used in the insulation of car door windows. The part is used in the driver's side door to shield water and other elements from entering the door where the window resides. Ford Motor has indicated that the part needs to be changed slightly for their 2001 model year automobiles. An extra amount of rubber will be applied to increase the part's ability to withstand stress. This change will result in two changes to the cost of the part, the material cost and the manufacturing cost. The old part cost $.03 per foot for material and $4 per foot for manufacturing and overhead. The year 2000 selling volume for the part was 48,000 feet for $284,000. The year 2001 projected sales are 52,000 feet.

1) Assuming that the part will be sold at a 5 percent decrease under 2000 selling prices, calculate how much the part should cost if the gross margin on the sale remains the same.

2) How many feet of material and at what price should the budget be set for part #47H59830-3 for the year 2001? Include any assumptions you need to make to arrive at the budgeted number.

**Part B**

The sales budget triggers the calculation of all other budgets, including the cost of goods sold and the raw materials budget. As shown in the sales forecast, one of this year's points of emphasis for the budget is completing the budget by December 31.

As cost accounting manager for RSC, Jeff Shultes is in a tough spot. Jeff's responsibilities include getting the budget completed on time, but he needs help from several departments. Most notably, Jeff needs new standard costs to be set by the industrial engineering department. The standard costs will then be used to create the cost of goods sold budget and the raw materials purchases budget.

Michelle Frost heads the industrial engineering department. Although Michelle knows the importance of completing the new standard costs on time to supply to the budget system, her department has hit a few snags. The new sales forecast includes several products that RSC has never manufactured before, requiring her people to create estimates of both raw material costs and manufacturing costs. Michelle has informed Jeff that information he needs will be late.

Jeff is in trouble. With only three days left until the deadline, his critical source of information is going to be late.

Organize into a team for this question. Assume you are members of the cost accounting department. Your task is to come up with suggestions and alternatives that Jeff can take to his boss to solve the problem with industrial engineering. Be creative, but remember that your final results will be shared with Jeff's boss.

Brainstorming List

Top 3 Recommendations

# Chapter 7

## Divisional Performance

Decision making in businesses is usually enhanced when the people closest to either the customer or the important business process have decision-making responsibility and authority. Growing businesses realize that part of their natural evolution is to break down decision making by creating separate divisions or units.

Once established, the new divisions need a system to keep their efforts on track with the needs of the overall organization. Issues such as profitability reporting for divisions, transfer pricing, and performance evaluation all must be faced and integrated into a management control system that helps the business fulfill corporate goals.

### *Assignment 7-A: Opening Case: Christi's Coffee and Cream*

Christi's Coffee and Cream is owned by Bob Corby. Bob opened his first store, named for his wife, in Cleveland in 1993. Spotting a trend where people were leaving the house in the morning without time to brew fresh coffee, Christi's drive-through lanes became very popular. Soon, the opportunity to expand turned into a growing business opportunity. By 1997, Bob had ten local Christi's Coffee and Cream stores in the Cleveland shore area.

Early in 1998, Bob was approached by several people who were interested in starting their own Christi's stores. Initially Bob rejected the idea. Later Bob realized that to grow his business any larger than the ten stores he personally managed would take a management team. Bob hired Mark Williams and Jeff Harley to run two new divisions, Christi's South and Christi's West. Each person began his business with one store and quickly expanded to three each.

Williams and Harley provided enthusiasm and dedication to Christi's during the first two years of running the South and West branches. In 2000, however, the business hit a snag. Sales and profits in the new branches had leveled off. Neither manager was interested in taking on new stores, even though the market potential was clearly there. Bob realized that something had to be done to jump-start the business.

Bob called in a team of local consultants to discuss the problem. Among the many things mentioned was the lack of a performance measurement system for the South and West divisions. Also mentioned was the lack of an incentive program to motivate Mark and Jeff to take on additional risks by expanding the number of stores under their control. Bob assured the consulting team that he would take their comments into consideration.

1) How important is a performance measurement system to keeping a growing business on track? Why?

2) What could Bob do to both motivate his employees and to increase sales and profits?

3) At Mark's store, the customers' favorite item is a special croissant made with a honey cinnamon coating. This item is so hot, Mark cannot bake enough, even though it is the highest gross margin product sold. Jeff has asked Mark to bake extra croissants for his stores as well. Mark will have to build another oven and hire an extra cook to make the product. After some negotiation, the price could not be determined. Both Mark and Jeff's performance are currently measured based on net income.

   a. What other alternatives to a negotiated price should Bob consider for Mark and Jeff's transfer price problem?

   ______________________________________________________________________

   ______________________________________________________________________

   ______________________________________________________________________

   ______________________________________________________________________

   ______________________________________________________________________

   ______________________________________________________________________

   ______________________________________________________________________

   ______________________________________________________________________

   b. What would be the impact on the business if the transfer price selected caused the overall profit contribution of Mark's business to suffer?

   ______________________________________________________________________

   ______________________________________________________________________

   ______________________________________________________________________

   ______________________________________________________________________

   ______________________________________________________________________

   ______________________________________________________________________

   ______________________________________________________________________

   ______________________________________________________________________

## *Assignment 7-B: Case Study: Bryant Berets*

Bryant Berets, a hat-making company located in New Hampshire, has several divisions. Division B produces two kinds of berets, model H3B and model Y9M. Division manager Kevin Jones recently reported the following results when asked for product line profitability:

## Bryant Berets

### Divisional Segment Margin

(amounts in dollars)

| | Division B | | Model H3B | | Model Y9M | |
|---|---|---|---|---|---|---|
| **Sales** | 900,000 | 100% | 500,000 | 100% | 400,000 | 100% |
| **Less Variable Expenses** | 585,000 | 65% | 350,000 | 70% | 235,000 | 58.80% |
| **Contribution Margin** | 315,000 | 35% | 150,000 | 30% | 165,000 | 41.25% |
| **Less Traceable Fixed Expenses** | 135,000 | 15% | 55,000 | 11% | 80,000 | 20% |
| **Product-line Segment Margin** | 180,000 | 20% | 95,000 | 19% | 85,000 | 21.25% |
| **Less Common Fixed Expenses** | 45,000 | 5% | | | | |
| **Divisional Segment Margin** | 135,000 | 15% | | | | |

Kevin is wondering about the impact of a possible 10 percent reduction in selling price for model Y9M. He is also curious about the impact of a new study that indicates that another 30 percent of his common fixed expenses can actually be traced directly to model H3B.

1) Assume that Bryant Berets reduces the selling price on model Y9M by 10 percent, resulting in a 15 percent increase in sales volume. Will divisional segment margin increase?

2) What is the potential impact on model H3B if the new report is correct about adding another 30 percent of the common fixed costs to the traceable fixed expenses? Will divisional segment margin change? Why or why not?

### *Assignment 7-C: Case Study: Sunny Music Company, MP3 Division*

Sunny Music Company, a large Asian-based company, has recently become aware of a growing trend of delivering music over the Internet in a format known as MP3. MP3, officials worry, has the potential to change forever the way music and videos are sold and distributed worldwide. Recent developments include the introduction of simple-to-operate recording and playback machines that allow for storage of music in digital form. The machines also permit recording and duplicating music without restrictions. This development has the potential to put music companies and music distributors out of business.

Additionally, the recent trend towards broadband Internet connection, where individuals will have access to high-speed connections permitting video and two-way interactions, seems to open up an unlimited number of potential business activities in the near future.

Sunny needs to be a leader in this field. A missed opportunity could mean the end of the company.

With this in mind, the officials at Sunny Music have decided to form a new division, called Sunny MP3 (SMP3), to explore the profit potential of this development. Internet-based, the SMP3 division is charged with signing talent, producing MP3 samples and full-length recordings, developing a Web site capable of delivering the product, and collecting fees for downloads. A separate budget for promotion of the site will be provided as well as an adequate budget to keep the Web site state of the art.

As consultants to this new and exciting enterprise, Sunny has charged your team with the development of a performance system that is in concert with the following goals:

- Become the worldwide leader in the delivery of online music, videos, and interactive products.
- Develop new products that utilize high-speed Internet connections.
- Create a reward system that will attract the best and the brightest people in the business for SMP3.

Realizing the importance of this new division, Sunny is willing to wait three years for the division to turn a profit. Funds will come from cash flows generated by the traditional side of Sunny's business.

**Background**

1) Go to www.mp3.com and investigate the MP3 format for delivering music over the Internet. Record your findings.

2) Go to www.Internet.com and, using the search tool, research MP3. Look for recent articles discussing the music industry's use of the MP3 format for digital music over the Internet. Also search for "broadband applications." Use the results to help predict the applications the SMP3 division will create. Record your findings.

3) Go to www.RealNetworks.com and look for evidence of support for the MP3 format. Record your findings.

**Assignments**

1) Develop a mission statement for the SMP3 division. Be sure to include the goals as stated by Sunny.

2) Create a performance measurement system for the SMP3 division. Include methods employed to hire and retain talented music and Web-experienced people.

3) What nonfinancial measurements are included in your performance management system? How important are the nonfinancial measurements to the success of the business? Explain.

4) What specific financial controls would you recommend for this division and why?

5) Determine what the division must do to keep abreast of developments in the industry. What impact should this activity have upon the performance measurement system?

________________________________________________________________

________________________________________________________________

________________________________________________________________

________________________________________________________________

________________________________________________________________

________________________________________________________________

________________________________________________________________

________________________________________________________________

**Team Assignments**

Prepare a four- to six-slide presentation on the performance measurement system for the division. Include financial and nonfinancial criteria. Present your findings in class.

Alternatively, prepare a 4- to 6-page recommendation report for the proposed performance measurement system. Include information on installation of the system.

### *Assignment 7-D: Case Study: Willow Watch Realty*

Willow Watch Realty is a small real estate company located in a small town in upstate New York. The company has been in existence for over 40 years. They have survived by having a strong customer focus and by treating their team of realtors well. The average length of service for their realtors is 25 years.

Recently, two of the younger and more aggressive agents left the agency to form their own company called New Generation Realty. New Generation hopes to carve a niche in the market for first-time homebuyers and younger couples moving to larger homes because of growing families. Initial market statistics of houses sold in Willow Watch's market indicate that the firm has already captured 25 percent of the first-time buyer market.

Willow Watch pays its agents on a straight commission basis. Experienced agents receive one-half of the commission generated on the sale of a typical home. Average selling price in the area is $150,000 at a 6 percent commission from the seller. The average sale represents a commission of $4,500 for the selling realtor. If the realtor is also responsible for listing the house for sale with the agency, an additional one percent, or $1,500, is earned by the agent.

Rumor has it that New Generation is offering their agents 3.6 percent, or a $5,400 commission, for the average $150,000 sale. This represents a 20 percent increase in commissions over what Willow Watch is paying. Willow Watch's president, Wil Tree, is worried. He wonders if the commission system that has worked well for 40 years needs to be reworked.

1) What role does money play in a compensation system? Is it a motivator, de-motivator, or both? Explain.

2) Describe the role rewards play in creating actions by employees that are in the best interests of a company.

3) Describe how the proposed increase in commissions could have a negative impact on Willow Watch Realty. Consider both the company's and the employees' point of view.

________________________________________________

________________________________________________

________________________________________________

________________________________________________

________________________________________________

________________________________________________

________________________________________________

________________________________________________

### *Assignment 7-E: Case Study: Brantford Paper Company, Inc.*

Brantford Paper Company, Inc. (BPC), is a wholly owned subsidiary of Wisconsin Paper, Inc., and is located in Brantford, Ontario, Canada. BPC produces the binding material used to adhere bindings to books. In addition to the material produced for Wisconsin Paper, the company has customers in Canada and around the world. Products shipped to the United States have recently come under review by both Revenue Canada and the U.S. Internal Revenue Service for possible transfer pricing irregularities.

Presently, BPC transfers binding materials on a cost-plus profit method that is the result of negotiations between the two companies. This has resulted in a transfer price that is lower than the amount charged to other Canadian customers and non-affiliated companies in the United States. The result of the transfer has been a steady loss shown by the Canadian BPC, which has resulted in lower taxes paid to Revenue Canada.

The current transfer price is $4.24 USD. The price charged to Canadian customers is $4.58 USD. Revenue Canada has requested that the transaction be re-priced taking an "arms-length" approach.

**Background**

- Read your textbook's presentation on international transfer pricing.
- Go to www.pwcglobal.com/ and look up the information about transfer pricing with the country of Canada. Use the Web site's internal search tool with the keywords "transfer pricing."

**Assignments**

1) What is an "arm's-length" approach to transfer pricing? How could the use of an arm's-length transfer pricing policy help gain acceptance from Revenue Canada for BPC's transfer price?

2) What transfer price should be used for the binding material and why? What factors should be considered in arriving at a good transfer price?

# Chapter 8

## Inventory Management

The proper management of inventory is a critical element in developing a competitive business. Companies with lower levels of inventory can create positive advantages over companies that carry high levels of inventory. The advantages are having less money tied up in inventory and discovering any potential quality problems sooner.

Inventory carries both raw material costs and costs of conversion. The money used to purchase the raw material and to purchase shop labor and overhead is locked up until the products can actually be sold. Companies that can turn inventory into cash faster will have more financial resources available to do other things for the company.

Inventory is a necessary evil. Companies need inventory. Inventory is the seed of the final product, the basic component of the transformation process. However, companies that find ways to substantially reduce inventory typically enjoy faster throughput cycles, shorter lead times from order date to ship date, and potentially higher levels of quality.

### *Assignment 8-A: Opening Story: Warwick Box Company*

Warwick Box Company is a small manufacturer of fancy cardboard boxes located in the heart of the Rhode Island jewelry manufacturing district. The Rhode Island jewelry industry is characterized by many small firms with 5 to 20 employees each. The jewelry manufacturers each produce a unique line of products for select distributors. The selling process consists of taking their creations, packaged in unique boxes, to distributors. Warwick Box Company manufactures the boxes.

John and Andy Spoltore jointly own Warwick Box Company. They have two full-time employees, and business over the years has been adequate. Presently, the company has plenty of cardboard (raw material inventory) and no cash in the bank. Several suppliers have placed the business on a cash basis. This means that Warwick Box Company must pay cash in advance to receive the materials they need to get the job done.

A consultant, Lee Chin, from the local office of the Small Business Development Center is called in to discuss the problem with John and Andy. Lee says, “John, when I look around the shop, I see hundreds of different types of cardboard on the shelves. Some of the cardboard has dust on the top piece. How many types of material do you carry in inventory?” “Well, Lee,” John responds, “we have had orders in the past for every piece of cardboard you see here. Sometimes we have to order in quantity to get a good price from the manufacturer. If the order falls through, we get stuck with the inventory. It’s just a normal cost of doing business." Andy adds, "Besides, if we didn't carry this inventory in stock, we couldn't respond quickly to emergency orders. Quick turnaround orders represent 20 percent of our sales."

Lee responds, "Yes, I see. How often does a quick turnaround order result in an order for unique material that you don't carry in stock?" "More than half the time," responded John. "John, what kind of premium do you get on those quick turnaround orders?" said Lee. "We get a 15 percent premium, but the customers are very slow to pay, taking 65 days on average." Lee responds, "So, the stock of specialty cardboard continues to grow and the customers are paying late. Sounds like the situation will only get worse."

1) Why is inventory a problem for Warwick Box Company?

2) What is the basic premise behind just-in-time (JIT) inventory?

3) Could JIT apply to Warwick Box Company? Why or why not?

4) As an inventory consultant, what would you recommend to the management of Warwick Box Company?

### *Assignment 8-B: Case Study: Tune Corporation Parts for Bicycle Racing*

Tune Corporation is based in Massachusetts, sells a system for measuring the amount of energy a bike rider is exerting during a workout. The product is sold to avid bicyclists who want an advantage during training. The premise is this: If you want to train to the maximum, you need to design workouts that push your body to the edge. Factors such as head wind, inclines, and road conditions all affect the quality of a workout. The Power Tap™ system provides athletes with a measure of the total energy generated while on a workout.

In a recent article, company president Gerhard Pawelka stated, "One of the reasons we chose to create a product for the parts and accessories market (is because) the margins are a lot better than in the basic metal and sculpting that goes into manufacturing bikes."[1] The Tune Corporation's main product, the Power Tap™ system, has four component parts: a computer, a hub, a heart rate monitor, and a receiver and mount. Each part is sold separately as a replacement part.

Product distribution is growing. The question facing Tune Corporation is how to best serve its customers.

Visit Tune Corporation at www.etune.com and

a. Find the list of current dealers.
b. Locate the current pricing for the system and the individual units.
c. Try the interactive demo.

1) Should the company build product in anticipation of sales or should it adapt a JIT system and wait for orders before beginning the manufacturing cycle? What factors will have the most impact on your decision?

________________________________________________________________

________________________________________________________________

________________________________________________________________

________________________________________________________________

________________________________________________________________

________________________________________________________________

________________________________________________________________

________________________________________________________________

________________________________________________________________

________________________________________________________________

________________________________________________________________

________________________________________________________________

________________________________________________________________

[1] M. A. Nelen, "Tune Corp. looking to 'PowerTap' into the bicycle racing market," *Mass High Tech*, Vol. 17, Issue 16, April 19-25, 1999, p. 3.

2) If the company installs JIT, what factors will need to be taken into consideration when Tune Corporation chooses their vendors for component parts?

_______________________________________________

_______________________________________________

_______________________________________________

_______________________________________________

_______________________________________________

_______________________________________________

_______________________________________________

_______________________________________________

_______________________________________________

### *Assignment 8-C: Case Study: W.B. Mason Office Products on the Net*

At first glance, W.B. Mason looks like the perfect business to be attracted to the Internet. The management of W.B. Mason agrees. The firm is a Boston-based office products distributor with 11 distribution centers in the Northeast but no consumer stores. Selling directly to businesses, orders come from the phone, fax, and postal (snail) mail. The management of W.B. Mason agrees.

Peter Dupre, chief information officer, recently stated, "We've been on the Net for about a year. One reason we got involved was to retain business, and we have done that. But it's turned into much more than that." He went on to say, "Our emphasis on on-line commerce is a key part of our overall strategy, because so many businesses are becoming active on the Web. Business to business purchasing (agents) aren't there to browse. They see inventory, compare prices and make purchases. We think we can do that better than our major competitors."[2]

Around 5 percent of total business is presently coming from the Web site, but that figure is expected to grow to 20-25 percent within one year's time. The entire catalogue of items available for sale is now a few clicks away on the company's Web site. User name and password is required, however. W.B. Mason does not sell to the public like Staples and Office Max does. The company offers free delivery of all products ordered.

Visit W.B. Mason at www.wbmason.com. Look for evidence of how they handle their inventory of products for sale.

---

[2] Dyke Hendrickson, "W.B. Mason Chooses Net Over Bricks," *Mass High Tech*, Vol. 17, Issue 16, April 19-25, 1999, p. 14.

1) W.B. Mason gives Guaranteed Overnight Local Delivery, or G.O.L.D. Star Service, for all orders placed with no minimums and no delivery charge. What kind of inventory system must they have in place to provide this service? Explain.

2) W.B. Mason is considering offering products for sale in California. What adjustments, if any, will they need to make to their G.O.L.D. service? What will be the impact on their inventory system, if any?

## *Assignment 8-D: Case Study: Amazing Books Online*

The Amazing Books Online company, an Internet based business, began in 1996. The online seller of books quickly became one of the most recognized names in the Internet industry. Customers loved the simplicity of having millions of books available for purchase right at their computer keyboards. Repeat customers accounted for over 35 percent of ongoing business.

The growth of the company presented management with some interesting problems. Online customers expect quick service. Shipment of orders within 48 hours is considered to be marginally acceptable. Customers would prefer shipment on the same day the order is submitted. The customer expectation has very demanding implications to the inventory management system.

Inventory for a bookseller consists of books. The ability to ship products within 48 hours depends on both the availability of the book and the ability of the system to locate, package, and deliver the book to a third-party delivery system such as United Parcel service or Federal Express. Inventory is classified into three categories: available for immediate shipment, ship within 2–3 days, and ship within 2 weeks. Immediate shipment is available for best sellers and other books that Amazing may be promoting at the time. Books in the 2–3 day classification are stored in a third-party book distributor's warehouse.

1) Calculate the economic order quantity for a book that sells 5,000 copies per 13-week period, has a unit carrying cost of $1.00, a setup cost of $50.00, and a lead time of 4 weeks.

2) If the company were to initiate a system of just-in-time, what would be different about the costs and the decisions made by management regarding the inventory for the book selling 5,000 copies per 13-week period?

3) How does selling over the Internet change the way companies look at inventory? What is different and why?

4) JIT systems typically place additional emphasis on both the delivery schedule of parts from a vendor and the levels of quality expected from the vendor. Is this emphasis any different for Amazing Books Online? Why or why not?

# Chapter 9

## Capital Investing Techniques

Project valuation of capital expenditures takes place on a number of levels. First, new capital projects are analyzed based upon the present value of projected cash flows. Projects that meet the company's financial requirements are then sent for approval within the organization. But what happens both before and after the analysis of the cash flows? This section seeks to document the project dynamics surrounding the numbers.

### The Capital Budgeting Process

The first step in the process of a company making a major capital expenditure is normally the capital budgeting process. Since not even Microsoft can do everything it may want to do at any given time, choices need to be made. (Note: Visit http://www.microsoft.com/msft/invest.htm for an updated list of Microsoft's recent major investments and acquisitions of companies.) In the fourth quarter of fiscal 1998, Microsoft's revenue was $4.0 billion, a 26 percent increase over the comparable quarter in fiscal 1997. For the quarter, net income was $1.36 billion, and earnings per share were $0.50, an increase of 25 percent compared to the $0.40 earned during the same quarter last year."[1] How does Microsoft decide what companies to buy and invest in?

According to Ross, Westerfield, and Jordan, the most fundamental decision process a business must make concerns its product line.[2] What products will it produce? What services will it offer? For Microsoft, consideration is also given to what technologies it must develop or acquire to remain the dominant software company in the industry. Technologies that either complement existing products and services or that threaten existing or future market share are strategically targeted for either development or acquisition.

For smaller companies, the process of deciding which projects to undertake is usually a simple process of developing, refining, and approving a "wish list" of potential projects. Projects that survive the initial cut are typically projects that complement the businesses strategic plan. The developing phase usually starts with a call from the executive office to submit a list of proposed capital projects for the upcoming year. The only financial information required in the initial phase is gross estimates of new sales potential or cost savings anticipated.

---

[1] Taken from the Microsoft Web site, http://www.microsoft.com, September 30, 1998.

[2] Ross, Westerfield, Jordan, *Fundamentals of Corporate Finance, 4th edition*, Irwin McGraw-Hill, Chicago: 1998, p. 232.

## *Assignment 9-A: Opening Story: Victor Controls Company*

Victor Controls Company (Victor) is a manufacturer of valves and flow control products for industrial pipelines. Located in central Iowa, Victor established a worldwide reputation for product excellence by providing a majority of the control valves for Saudi Arabia's vast oil fields in the 1960s. In the 1970s, the company expanded into manufacturing valves for the then-growing nuclear power plant business. Built from sound, well-engineered products and backed by an industry-unique manufacturer's representative system, Victor experienced double-digit growth throughout the 1960s and 1970s.

The system used by Victor for the approval of new capital expenditures was fairly simple. Each year, the management team was required to submit input to the capital budget. Projects were proposed, categorized, and prioritized. The highest rated projects were included in the yearly capital plan. Project ranking was based upon (a) the fit to strategic plan, (b) the need to sustain existing sales, and (c) markets and new market opportunities.

Project analysis consisted first of determining project cash flows. On a replacement project, where an asset such as a machine tool would be taken out of service and replaced with a new one, the criteria for approval were simple. First, a project needed to be on the capital budget list or a special exception memo needed to be attached to the project justification. Second, a project needed to achieve a positive net present value (NPV), discounted at 15 percent. In addition, a project needed an internal rate of return (IRR) approaching 20 percent and a payback of less than five years.

The project analysis team consisted of an industrial engineer, a manufacturing manager or supervisor, a financial analyst, and a purchasing agent. A project authority for expenditure (PAFE) form was completed and authorized signatures were obtained based upon the dollar amount of expenditure that various managers could approve. For example, expenditures greater than $100,000 required approval by the vice-president.

When the preliminary numbers did not meet the targets established in the budget process, or when established target rates for NPV, payback, and IRR were not met, the project was handed back to the project team for analysis. If the project had the support of the manufacturing organization, the industrial engineer took another look at the underlying assumptions driving the cost justification of the project. Often, the engineer "revised" the numbers with either lower costs or higher revenue that would exceed Victor's internal targets for a successful project.

One of the roles of the financial analyst was to keep the entire team honest. The analyst needed to verify the capital project hardware estimates, the cost justifications, and the proposed length of the project. Each team member realized, however, that the financial analyst would be revisiting or auditing the project for actual performance a year after purchase. The management team would hold the team responsible for underperforming capital projects.

1) How strong is this system of project evaluation? Does it encourage risk taking? Does it promote teamwork? Give examples.

2) Will Victor's system result in the best project being chosen for completion? Why or why not?

3) What do you think will happen to a project that has great financial numbers but lacks support from the organization? Why?

4) Can you suggest changes that might improve Victor's capital budgeting process?

______________________________________________________________________

______________________________________________________________________

______________________________________________________________________

______________________________________________________________________

______________________________________________________________________

______________________________________________________________________

### *Assignment 9-B (advanced), 9-C (basic): Case Study: West End Manufacturing*

*Note: This case can be completed by a group or by individuals.*

West End Manufacturing is a manufacturer of tools for the automotive industry. Many of the tools it manufactures require precision machine grinding or stamping of metal parts. Each year, a portion of their capital budget is set aside for replacement of machine tools.

**Project Task:** Replace a machine tool with a new model, achieving cost savings and X percent sales growth potential.

**Roles:** Engineer, accountant, manufacturing supervisor, materials coordinator, sales manager, and purchasing agent. (Note: For smaller teams, manufacturing can combine with materials and sales can combine with purchasing.)

**Group dynamics:** The manufacturing or materials team member will be responsible for presenting the project for the approval by management. The report will include all cost figures, product information, a brief technical explanation of how the new machine tool will work, and any other data deemed relevant to the decision. Team members need to defend their own input to the project.

**Data:** The original machine cost $135,000 when purchased in 1989. A 10-year life using MACRS depreciation was used. Salvage value is $10,000. The old machine tool is used to support $90,000 in sales per year. Material and labor are costs 65 percent of sales. The corporate tax rate is 35 percent. The new machine, purchased in 2000, costs $400,000 with an estimated useful life of 10 years. In addition to the $90,000 in sales that the new machine will support, the company is looking to add an additional $28,000 in expansion market sales per year. Initial estimates indicate that the new machine will carry a cost structure of 60 percent material and labor costs compared to sales. The company uses a 15 percent hurdle rate for replacement projects and a 20 percent rate for sales expansion projects. Calculation of NPV, IRR, and payback are required.

**Requirements for 9-B:** This project will require each team member to participate in the creation of the project proposal.

**Prepare:**

1) A detailed sales forecast for existing and expansion market sales that the new machine will support.
2) A cost estimate for the individual components of the project.
3) Information relative to product quality, ability to manufacture, and impact on inventories and shop floor workflows.
4) Detailed estimates of the machine tools under consideration, highlighting their unique features.
5) An inventory impact statement detailing the cash flow impact for carrying additional inventory.
6) A five-year analysis of cash flows created by the project.
7) Calculate the project's NPV, IRR, and payback.

**Requirements for 9-C:** The project will require each team member to participate in the creation of the project proposal.

**Prepare:**

1) A detailed sales forecast for existing and expansion market sales that the new machine will support.
2) A cost estimate for the individual components of the project.
3) The financial analyst will prepare a five-year analysis of cash flows created by the project.
4) A presentation for both financial and team data including project cash flows, NPV, IRR, and payback. Include the team's assessment of the most important nonfinancial elements of the project.

### *Assignment 9-D: Peggy's Cove: Comparing Alternatives in a Government Environment*

The village of Peggy's Cove, Nova Scotia, is facing a dilemma regarding the capital budget. Tourism, the number one industry for the village, needs to be continually supported with improvements/repairs to the infrastructure. Road repair, street lighting, maintenance of the lighthouse, and trash removal all require constant attention and money. This year, the village council is considering two major projects, a parking lot and a tax abatement request from a business that wants to expand. The village cannot afford both projects; it must choose one or the other.

**Case for the parking lot.** Peggy's Cove is a sleepy fishing village with many sea-battered cottages and lighthouses located on a picturesque Atlantic Ocean shore. Tourists come mainly from Halifax by car to tour the seacoast, look at the buildings, and spend money in the village's many shops. With only one entrance to the village, traffic can be a problem at times during the busy summer season. Visitors who cannot find adequate parking sometimes leave Peggy's Cove without spending any time or money. An additional parking lot, with shuttle service from approximately two miles from the village center, would handle all overflow traffic and preserve the nature of the village.

The cost for the parking lot is estimated to be $250,000, with an additional cost of $40,000 for the purchase of two shuttle vans, ongoing maintenance, gas and oil, and labor of $8,000 per month during the busy season. Additional tax revenue to cover the expenditures will come from a 2 percent additional sales tax on all purchases within the village. Estimated additional tax revenue each year is expected to be $197,000 in the first year and grow by 8 percent per year for the next seven years.

**Case for tax abatement.** East Bay Clothing, a regional retailer of outdoor clothes located in Bangor, Maine, has proposed a new store for Peggy's Cove. Occupying over 4,000 square feet, the proposed store would become the largest retail outlet in the village. The building proposal would keep the same theme and style of existing buildings and be built on a vacant lot near the center of the village. East Bay is looking for tax abatements in consideration for building the new retail store. Its contention is that the new store will draw more visitors into the village, creating more overall spending at the existing shops in the village. East Bay is asking for a tax-free first five years, which will cost the village approximately $200,000. The additional tax revenue due to the village from the other stores in the area is difficult to determine but should amount to $20,000 per year.

**Group Dynamics:** The stakeholders in this situation are many. Village residents are anti-development of any kind. The storeowners do not want to give a large retailer a foothold in their territory, especially when the big guy is getting a break. The village maintenance personnel are eager to expand their roles in the town. The town council men and women represent both the people who live and work in town and the businesses. Successful conclusion of this case will require excellent communications, negotiation skills, cross-functional teamwork, and realistic compromise.

**Background:** Visit http://www.yorkteam.com/tet.htm for ideas on getting more performance out of your project team.

**Project Tasks and Roles:** Assume one of the following roles and present your case to the village governing board: (A) town financial planner, (B) representative of the village's road maintenance department who will be in charge of building and maintaining the parking lot, or (C) a financial officer representing East Bay Clothing. Once a role has been determined, prepare a written report, with supporting schedules, presenting your position on which alternative should be pursued and why.

**Alternative #1:** Present the case in a "town meeting" environment where everyone has a chance to have his/her voice heard. Appoint a three-member town council to hear the arguments.

**Alternative #2:** Use the class as the town council and have the three representatives make their pitches for acceptance. Allow only one alternative to succeed.

### *Assignment 9-E: Case Study: Ultra-Light Software*

**Introduction:** Ultra-Light Software is a company with a long history of getting very close to bankruptcy only to be saved by a hot new product. The most recent balance sheet is provided on the next page. Ultra-Light needs help again. Two recent projects focusing on the business application side of the Internet have failed to sell in numbers large enough to re-coup their original investment. Time is short and a new idea must be developed, de-bugged, and generate sales by the end of the fiscal year.

Tom Terrific, a crackerjack programmer, has an idea. He would like Ultra-Light to buy out his company, the 10 G-Force Software Group, and acquire 10 G-Force's portfolio of software games as well as the current game development portfolio. Ultra-Light's management team is hesitant. They know nothing about the gaming software business and are a little hesitant to stake the company's future on this type of venture.

**Project Details:** The asking price for 10 G-Force is $1,300,000, but management feels the company can be purchased in a stock swap requiring no additional debt for Ultra-Light. Ongoing revenues from 10 G-Force are expected to be $800,000 per year with earnings before taxes of $180,000. New products in development have the following estimated probabilities for adding additional earnings before taxes this year and will grow by 15 percent per year for the following three years.

| | | | |
|---|---|---|---|
| Probability | 10% | ($50,000) | Loss |
| | 15% | $30,000 | Gain |
| | 30% | $40,000 | Gain |
| | 45% | $20,000 | Gain |

Typically, projects are evaluated using discounted cash flow techniques with a minimum acceptance rate of 12 percent. Last year the company achieved a 14 percent on equity. Management feels that 10 G-Force, because of the unique risk they bring to the company, should be discounted at 20 percent for evaluation purposes.

**Group Dynamics:** This is a project that needs to be sold to the board of directors on more than just the numbers. The graphic violence depicted in 10 G-Force software games introduces an ethical element to Ultra-Light's decision to buy Tom Terrific's company. A team representative should assume the role of the marketing department and assess the potential for selling the controversial software. Expect resistance from the board of directors. Traditional software product lines have emphasized such staples as company-wide e-mail programs and networking software. Team reports, delivered either in writing or in person, should address both the nature of the gaming market and clearly identify the risks.

**Recent Balance Sheet:**

ULTRA-LIGHT, Inc.
CONSOLIDATED BALANCE SHEETS
(in thousands, except share data)

| | March 31, 1999 |
|---|---|
| ASSETS | |
| Current assets: | |
| Cash and cash equivalents | $ 17,876 |
| Marketable securities | 14,854 |
| Net accounts receivable | 22,717 |
| Prepaid expenses and other current assets | 2,160 |
| Total current assets | 57,607 |
| Property, plant, and equipment, at cost: | |
| Computers and office equipment | 15,013 |
| Leasehold improvements | 5,379 |
| Land and building | 4,200 |
| Furniture and fixtures | 2,130 |
| Total property and equipment | 26,722 |
| Less: Accumulated depreciation and amortization | 12,152 |
| Net property and equipment | 14,570 |
| Long-term marketable securities | 710 |
| Intangible assets, net | 10,906 |
| Other assets | 1,372 |
| | $ 85,165 |

LIABILITIES AND STOCKHOLDERS' EQUITY

| | |
|---|---|
| Current liabilities: | |
| Line of credit | $ 10,350 |
| Note payable | 25,000 |
| Accounts payable | 2,329 |
| Accrued expenses | 11,698 |
| Deferred revenues | 4,719 |
| Current maturities of long-term obligations | 96 |
| Total current liabilities | 54,192 |
| Long-term obligations, net of current maturities | 22,764 |
| Stockholders' equity: | |
| Preferred stock, $.10 par value | |
| Authorized - 2,000,000 shares | |
| Issued and outstanding - none | |
| Common stock, $.001 par value | |
| Authorized - 100,000,000 shares; | |
| Issued and outstanding - 35,785,000 shares at March 31, 1999 | 36 |
| Additional paid-in capital | 142,530 |
| Accumulated deficit | (134,357) |
| Total stockholders' equity | 8,209 |
| | $ 85,165 |

1) Prepare an analysis of the cash flows expected from the investment in 10 G-Force software. Should Ultra-Light purchase 10 G-Force? Will it achieve enough cash flow from the acquisition to hold off bankruptcy? Be sure to include marketing information about the software gaming industry.

2) Track all team communications and file a separate report. Be sure to have every team member rate the team on how well they feel the team communicated. Include a list of suggestions for improving communication on the next team you participate on.

_______________________________________________

_______________________________________________

_______________________________________________

_______________________________________________

_______________________________________________

_______________________________________________

_______________________________________________

_______________________________________________

_______________________________________________

_______________________________________________

_______________________________________________

_______________________________________________

## *Assignment 9-F: Case Study: Turning Ash into Gold: Finding an Economically Sound Alternative for Waste*

For centuries, power companies have converted minerals extracted from the earth into fuel. The most common method used has been burning coal to produce electrical power. The burning of coal creates, as a by-product, heavy amounts of a white, powdery substance called ash. In most cases, the majority of ash becomes airborne in the smokestacks of the power plant, polluting the air and then the land in the surrounding area. Modern plants, however, have begun to capture the ash in the smokestacks before the substance becomes airborne. To clean the substance from smokestacks, ground limestone is combined with water and then sprayed into the smokestacks, removing sulfur dioxide from the smoke. The result is toothpaste-like substance caller scrubber sludge.

Dr. Summer Malcolm from the University of Alabama has suggested a new use for this former waste product. He suggests that the power companies either sell the scrubber sludge to farmers as a fertilizer or sell the material to construction material companies for the production of wallboard.[3]

EcoBuild, LLC, is a new company focusing on taking materials normally discarded from industrial processes or natural material and converting them into ecologically sound

[3] *Wall Street Journal*, October 5, 1998, p. B1.

building materials. Early experiments with straw and with ash have proven to be both economical to build and ecologically safe.

**Project Details:** The chief financial officer has asked your cross-functional team for input on a major decision facing your company in the next few months. EcoBuild has secured a contract to build low-income houses for people who could not otherwise afford housing. The costs will be paid for by an international foundation, but the total cost for the project must be kept to a minimum. Your team's task is to determine whether to fabricate the material for the house on site or make the material at the main factory and incur shipping costs.

**The Process:** The in-house manufacturing process for manufacturing ash-based wallboard is as follows. The ash is combined with air shot into the mixture at a very high pressure. The mixture is then forced into molds crafted especially for the house under construction. Computer controls, entered at the factory to the exact specifications of the house under construction, ensure the correct output from the process. The cost of new computer equipment and the equipment to fabricate building pieces is $300,000. The equipment can be sent to a job site and set up for an additional $10,000. Flatbed trucks will haul finished material from the main site to the remote locations for $1.75 per mile. Five truckloads will be needed to completely deliver enough material for one house. Shipping damage is estimated to add another $5,000 per home if the miles to the job site exceed 1,000.

**The Project:** Currently under consideration is a group of ten houses, located in Arizona, all selling for $150,000 per contract. Gross margin is 50 percent of sales revenue. Arizona is approximately 1,500 miles from the main factory. Five flatbed trucks can haul the materials required to build one home. Sales of similar houses in the area have been fairly steady at 500 starts per year over the past five years.

1) Determine whether or not EcoBuild should make the order at the plant or build another manufacturing facility in Arizona. The project justification will require input from a marketing representative on the feasibility of continued sales in the Arizona area. Discuss the advantages and disadvantages of each approach.

2) Prepare a slide show for presentation to the chief financial officer of EcoBuild. Outline your slide show here.

______________________________________________

______________________________________________

______________________________________________

______________________________________________

______________________________________________

______________________________________________

### *Assignment 9-G: Case Study: Liquor Store Blues: Sell to Local College or Not?*

The Jonesfield Liquor store is located on a busy road approximately four miles from a suburban college campus. The short distance to the store has made Jonesfield a popular place for students to purchase beer and wine. Local business is fairly steady, with year-to-year store sales growing at a modest 5 percent per year, mostly due to increases in lottery sales.

The storeowners are concerned about a trend, however. On weekend nights between 5:00 and the closing time of 9:00 PM, they are seeing more students and less town residents. Most of the students are purchasing large quantities of alcohol and behaving in a loud manor. Local residents are not to be found during these times. In addition, undercover police looking for underage buyers of alcohol have frequented the store, which is located within one mile from the Jonesfield police station. It is estimated that over 50 percent of students purchasing alcohol are using fake IDs.

**The Team:** Your team is made up of a financial analyst, a marketing researcher, a town representative, and a member of the local police force. Your team is to report back to the owner on how he should approach sales of alcohol to college students. One of the recommendations could possibly be closing the store and starting another business.

**The Numbers:** Since the sales of alcohol and tobacco to minors under the age of 21 is illegal in the state, Jonesfield has no choice but to carefully card everyone under the age of 30 for proper identification. Sales of beer and wine constitute 60 percent of the gross revenue for the store and 40 percent of the gross profit. If sales to college students were to cease, the store would see sales volume drop below break even.

**The Meeting:** Your group is to have a meeting where all parties identified above are represented. Minutes (detailed notes) from the meeting are to be taken. The minutes of the meeting will serve as your completion of the assignment. Be sure to include the legal and ethical considerations brought up in the meeting in your report. Full meeting minutes should appear here.

# Chapter 10

## World-Class Manufacturing

The road to world-class manufacturing is paved with excellence. According to World Class Manufacturing Enablers, a definition of world-class manufacturing is to "manufacture products profitably, (and to) provide better value than the competition."[1] Top management needs to express a clear vision and an environment that will allow people to achieve their best. Middle managers need to coach, teach, and provide resources. Line supervisors need to support employees, empower employees to excel, and act as facilitators.

The need for management accountants to participate in the process of continuously improving both the systems and the people who run them is strongly evident. Not only does this environment provide measurement challenges, but it also challenges people to accept change as a normal way of doing business. New measurement techniques must be developed that include working closely with every member of the company's team.

Traditional function-based measurement systems can not only fail to give correct answers for companies who are well on their way to world-class manufacturing, but they also can provide reasons for not making needed changes.

### *Assignment 10-A: Opening Story: Javad Positioning Systems & SMT Centre Inc.*

Javad Positioning Systems assembles global positioning systems under ISO 9000 standards.[2] The resulting products enable a user to determine his or her exact (within 1 to 100 meters) positioning anywhere on this planet. The devices are used by governments for military applications, by businesses for surveying and to determine where people and equipment such as delivery trucks are located, and by people to determine directions.

The products require a level of precision manufacturing seldom found in most goods. This is because any slight error in sending or receiving a signal from the high earth orbit satellite system will cause a distortion in the positioning accuracy. The Javad

---

[1] World Class Manufacturing Enablers Web site, http://wc-enablers.org/, visited on 6/5/99.

[2] ISO 9000 Standards can be found at http://www.iso.ch/, the home of the International Organization for Standardization. From the Web site: "ISO 9000 and ISO 14000 are practical tools to assist users in business and government to assure the quality of their products and services, and to manage the impact of their activities on the environment," visited on 6/5/99.

Positioning System claims accuracy to the thickness of a coin using satellites over 20,000 kilometers away.[3]

Manufacturing for Javad Positioning Systems is handled by SMT Centre Inc., a Canadian-based company with manufacturing facilities in Canada, the United States, Mexico, China, and Ireland. All plants are ISO 9000 certified. The company has won various awards for excellence. See the press release below.

> Toronto, Canada (September 23, 1998) -- The Surface Mount Technology Centre Inc. ("SMTC") for the second year running received industry recognition in service excellence, The *1998 Service Excellence Awards for Contract Electronics Manufacturers* were recently held in San Jose, CA and participating for the second time, SMTC received an award for **Value for Price** in the large company category. The company won in this category with an average score of 8.57, based on a rating scale of 1 to 10, with 10 being the highest.
>
> This is the only contest for contract electronics manufacturers in which the customers themselves rate suppliers in various service areas. Paul Walker, SMTC President, commented that, "SMTC is delighted to continue to be recognized by its customers for excellence in its manufacturing services. Again, we thank our customers for taking the time to participate. The depth of the survey provides our business teams with an excellent evaluation of our services and a benchmark for continuous improvement."[4]

SMTC is a dedicated user of teams and teamwork. Accordingly, the company has organized by customers, with traditional departments practically non-existent. "Our TOPS team is empowered and experienced to make the necessary decisions in real time. By understanding the needs of one customer, your TOPS team utilize the site and corporate resources available to them, so that they may truly provide continuous improvement in quality, manufacturing processes, cycle time reduction and value for price."[5]

---

[3] "GPS technology is relatively young but very complex. With GPS we measure very long distances accurate to the thickness of a coin, using weak signals of satellites that are 20,000 kilometers far. The challenge is to achieve good results not only under favorable conditions but also when the world is not perfect. Our research resulted in a new plateau of GPS technology (with 10 pending patents)." Taken from http://www.javad.com/Technology/index.html, visited on 6/5/99.

[4] http://www.smtc.com/smtc_homepage.nsf/30c877d348e440d3852566b4006cf021/9f4ade384cbb487b052566b500104a77?OpenDocument, visited on 6/5/99.

[5] http://www.smtc.com/smtc_homepage.nsf/30c877d348e440d3852566b4006cf021/27d29aba7f98aa93052566b500101960?OpenDocument, visited on 6/5/99.

1) Javad Positioning Systems outsources the manufacturing of its products to SMTC. How could a company that requires such a high level of quality trust another company to manufacture its products?

2) What can Javad do to improve the quality of its products? Address both internal issues and outsourcing issues.

3) SMTC is organized by customer-focused teams. What implications does this have to the process of allocating overhead costs?

4) SMTC, as described above, focuses on continuous improvement in quality, the manufacturing process, cycle time reduction, and giving value for price. How can costs be measured in a system that is constantly changing?

______________________________________________________________________

______________________________________________________________________

______________________________________________________________________

______________________________________________________________________

______________________________________________________________________

______________________________________________________________________

### *Assignment 10-B: Case Study: Borg-Warner Automotive*

Borg-Warner Automotive is a manufacturer of transmission bands, which facilitates the shifting of gear ratios in an automobile. From a 240,000-square-foot plant in Frankfort, Illinois, the company supplies more than half of North America's supply of transmission bands. Winner of the prestigious Industry Week's America's Best Plants award,[6] the plant is an outstanding example of how to succeed using modern manufacturing techniques.

The 490 employees practice constraint management. Employees continuously seek ways to eliminate the processes that constrain the flow of the manufacturing process. The results have been very good. Over the last five years, days inventory on hand has been reduced by 64.3 percent.[7]

The workforce is divided into four teams, each focused on a major subcategory of transmission bands produced by the plant. The teams are truly cross-functional, with members from manufacturing to design engineering to finance. The design of the teams allows a team to tackle any business issue that may come up. The major issues tend to focus on scrap, spending issues, and process constraints.

All major processes are measured and improvements are worked on religiously. Teams are taught to recognize and resolve the team's top issue, then go after the one that replaces it at the top of the list. This one-at-a-time focus really gets results. Manufacturing yields have improved by better than 30 percent over the last two years.[8]

---

[6] For more information on the Industry Week America's best plants award, see http://www.industryweek.com/iwinprint/bestplants/. Visited on 6/6/99.
[7] Borg-Warner Automotive, by George Taninecz, Industry Week Web site, http://www.industryweek.com/iwinprint/bestplants/bp_profiles.asp?Input=8, visited on 6/6/99.
[8] Ibid.

Visit http://www.industryweek.com/iwinprint/bestplants/bp_profiles.asp?Input=8 for information on this 1998 winner of Industry Week's Best Plant in America contest. Look for examples of world-class manufacturing.

Visit http://www.benchnet.com/datproc.htm to learn more about benchmarking.

1) The theory of constraints identifies five steps to achieve its goal of improving organizational performance. What are these five steps and how do they apply to Borg-Warner Automotive?

2) The major binding constraint is often called the *drummer*.[9] Assume that you are a member of the Borg-Warner transmission band team and you have identified the rubber molding operation as your drummer. Specify how this information will affect other decisions about inventory flowing into and out of this process.

3) A *time buffer* is the inventory that is established in front of the major binding constraint.[10] What is the time buffer's role in the drum-buffer-rope system? What impact would a 25 percent reduction in the time buffer have on total process time?

4) What are *ropes* and how do they control work-in-process inventory levels? What is the objective of a rope?

[9] Don Hansen and Maryanne Mowen, *Management Accounting, 5th Ed.*, South-Western College Publishing, Cincinnati, Ohio, 2000, p. 802.
[10] Ibid. p. 802.

5) Kelis Thacker, former plant manager at Borg-Warner Automotive, said, "You can set up your plant or business 10 different ways, and you can be successful all 10 different ways, if you've got the whole team on board,. If you've got the trust, respect in the organization, and the leadership, you can be successful."[11] Explain how teamwork can have a major impact on world-class manufacturing.

______________________________________________________________________

______________________________________________________________________

______________________________________________________________________

______________________________________________________________________

______________________________________________________________________

______________________________________________________________________

______________________________________________________________________

### *Assignment 10-C: Case Study: Implementing the Balanced Scorecard at Colorado Mine Co. Steakhouse*

Colorado Mine Co. Steakhouse (CMCS) is a successful brew-pub located in downtown Denver, Colorado. The two-floor building has room for over 200 patrons and a full dinner menu featuring steak and plenty of micro-brewed beer manufactured inside the building. Loyal customers enjoy a mixture of quality food, prompt service, rustic atmosphere, and plenty of fresh-brewed beer. Business is particularly busy whenever the Colorado Rockies have a home game, as CMCS is located just a few blocks from Coors Stadium.

CMCS strives to be the premiere eating and drinking location for the 21-to-35 crowd. Named the best brew-pub of 1995, the company strives to maintain its best-in-class reputation by constantly asking customers for feedback on both the quality of food and drink and service. A one-month training period for all new service associates (bartenders, wait staff) doubles as an evaluation period to weed out underperformers. Management believes that they can maintain their best-in-class status only by continuously improving everything they do.

The management of CMCS has seen both the customer base and the dollars spent rise over the last few years since opening of the new baseball stadium in 1994. Recently, however, the average dollars spent per patron has slipped. The result has been a reduction in the growth rate of both sales and profits within the business. The management team is concerned about the trend and has asked your firm, Student Consultants, Inc., to suggest ways to increase the company's sales and profits.

---

[11] Borg-Warner Automotive, by George Taninecz, Industry Week Web site, http://www.industryweek.com/iwinprint/bestplants/bp_profiles.asp?Input=8, visited on 6/6/99.

Your company is considered an expert in the Denver area in the implementation of the balanced scorecard. Your assignment is to assess the situation and bring your expertise to a proposed solution for the management of CMCS.

Visit http://www.balancedscorecard.com and http://www.balancedscorecard.org for more supplemental information on the balanced scorecard.

1) What are the four perspectives of the balanced scorecard and how do they relate to CMCS?

2) How would you define the strategic direction of Colorado Mine Co. Steakhouse? How important is a clear strategy to the development of the balanced scorecard?

3) How would you design a measurement for customer satisfaction? How will you align this measurement with the company strategy?

4) Develop a set of core objectives and measures for CMCS regarding the preparation and delivery of food to customers. Be sure to align these objectives with the overall strategy for the company.

### *Assignment 10-D: Case Study: Valmet Corporation: ISO 9000 and the Malcolm Baldrige Award*

Valmet is the world's leading supplier of paper and board machinery and related process control equipment. The company's leading technology and global network create products and services that are in demand all over the world. In order to maintain the highest levels of quality, Valmet has undertaken a systematic improvement to quality by striving to meet the quality standards set in the Malcolm Baldrige National Quality Award[12] and by qualifying for ISO 9000 certification.[13]

Both measurements attempt to establish procedures and measurements focused on continuous quality measurement based upon customer satisfaction and achieved results. Valmet has been adapting its quality operations to the Malcolm Baldrige National Quality Award for several years.[14] Continuous improvement, benchmarking, and measurements of all key processes are cornerstones of the system.

What are standards? Standards are documented agreements to technical specifications or other precise criteria that help establish a set of common expectations for performance when the standards are uniformly applied. A national quality award uses standards for performance that, when applied, will result in excellence in performance for goods and services produced.

Visit the corporate Web site at http://www.valmet.com.
Malcolm Baldrige National Quality Award information can be obtained at http://www.asq.org/abtquality/awards/baldrige.html.
ISO information can be obtained at http://www.iso.ch/welcome.html.

1) What is the worldwide significance of attaining a globally recognized quality standard such as ISO 9000? Can reaching ISO 9000 certification help sales? Why?

______________________________________________

______________________________________________

______________________________________________

______________________________________________

______________________________________________

______________________________________________

______________________________________________

______________________________________________

[12] Malcolm Baldrige National Quality Award information can be found at http://www.asq.org/abtquality/awards/baldrige.html.
[13] See http://www.iso.ch/welcome.html for ISO 9000 information, visited on 6/6/99.

2) Organizations that undertake quality programs strive for continuous improvement. What effect does a continuous reduction in manufacturing costs have on the company's managerial control system?

3) Can a traditional function-based cost system give a company wrong answers if the company is routinely reducing costs and improving throughput? If so, how is this possible?

[14] See http://www.valmet.com/news/1998mar2.htm, visited on 6/6/99.

# Chapter 11

## Value Chain Analysis

Value chain analysis involves looking at the whole picture of value creation from the final customer back to the initial raw material. As stated by Morse, Davis, and Hartgraves, "All entities are dependent on the final customer's perception of the value and cost of a product or service ... Consequently, the goal of every organization should be to maximize the value while minimizing the cost of a product or service to final customers."[1]

The unique perspective of the final customer gives every aspect of creating products and services new meaning and relevance. Each operation, process, added step, etc., must be examined under the light of the value created for the final customer. If operations or procedures do not add value to the final product, they become targets for reduction or elimination. All participants in the value chain must participate or unnecessary costs will end up in the final product or service.

### *Assignment 11-A: Opening Story: Sainsbury Supermarket's Supplier-Chain Initiative*

Sainsbury's, a leading United Kingdom grocery chain founded in 1869, opened its first store in Drury Lane, London, with the promise of "highest quality at keenest prices." In 1998, with around 400 stores in the United Kingdom, Ireland, and the United States, and total sales of £11.6 billion, Sainsbury's is still bringing the best products and high service quality to an increasing number of consumers.[2]

Due to the competitive nature of selling a commodity such as groceries, constant promotions are a way of life. Ten percent of all sales are a direct result of supplier-tied-in sales. At any one time, as many as 2,000 separate promotions may be running. Each promotion requires coordination with suppliers and delivery services. From 6-packs of Coke to 2-for-1 deals on packaged chicken, the ability of the supermarket chain to co-ordinate activity up and down the supplier chain is critical.

A well-run promotion has the potential to increase sales in the other 90 percent of sales categories as shoppers looking for bargains purchase other essential items. However, if the item promoted is out of stock, sales of other items also drop. Customers who wanted sale items are usually not in the mood to spend money after being disappointed.

---

[1] Wayne J. Morse, James R. Davis, Al L. Hartgraves, *Management Accounting, A Strategic Approach*, South-Western College Publishing, Cincinnati, Ohio, 1996, p. 169.

[2] Sainsbury Supermarkets: Case Study. Author unknown. Taken from http://www.microsoft.com/products/backoffice/dns/ecommerce/Sainsbur.htm, visited on 6/9/99.

To improve communications with suppliers, Sainsbury moved its paper-based catalogue to the Internet. A good first step, the company realized savings by being able to immediately post new items to the Web site. Recently, the company has added real-time collaborations features that permit suppliers to participate directly in promotions. For example, if Sainsbury elects to run a hot dog, chips, and buns promotion, the suppliers can check levels of inventory on the shelves and in warehouses before deciding how much additional stock to ship to the store. The results have been fewer stock-outs of promotion items, resulting in higher sales with no increases in inventory carrying costs. Visit http://www.microsoft.com/products/backoffice/dns/ecommerce/Sainsbur.htm.

1) How important is the supplier value chain for Sainsbury Supermarkets? How many major processes can you find in the information above?

______________________________________________

______________________________________________

______________________________________________

______________________________________________

______________________________________________

______________________________________________

2) What is the impact to the value chain if the chicken supplier is paying too much money for storage costs?

______________________________________________

______________________________________________

______________________________________________

______________________________________________

______________________________________________

3) What is the impact to Sainsbury Supermarkets if a supplier sends contaminated merchandise directly to the shelves of the market?

______________________________________________

______________________________________________

______________________________________________

______________________________________________

______________________________________________

## *Assignment 11-B: Case Study: VerticalNet.com, Web-based Vertical Trading Communities*

VerticalNet, Inc., is one of many growing sites on the Internet that pulls together companies that have a lot in common. VerticalNet is the Internet's leading creator and operator of vertical trade communities. VerticalNet leverages the interactive features and global reach of the Internet to create multinational, targeted business-to-business communities. These narrowly focused Web sites attract buyers and sellers from around the world by catering to individuals with similar professional interests.

The major attraction is the pulling together into one Web site the businesses and services that might have to be sought out individually. The success of the formula will be determined by the quality of the information, services, and sense of community generated by the VerticalNet Web sites. As in other aspects of business, companies forge relationships with proven performers. On the Internet, collections of proven performers help to create instant, worldwide markets.

ChemicalOnline.com, for example, contains edited information about recent news events, job openings, online auctions, and targeted advertisements. Companies in the chemical industry can choose this one source for products and services with some assurances that the products offered for sale have been approved by the staff of the Web site. Companies can even auction surplus equipment or check out the latest industry news.

- Visit http://www.verticalnet.com for a look at all vertical communities available on the Web site. Look for evidence of gathering similar companies within industries.

1) How does the concept of a vertical industry focus Web site further the concept of managing the vertical chain?

___________________________________________________________________________

___________________________________________________________________________

___________________________________________________________________________

___________________________________________________________________________

___________________________________________________________________________

___________________________________________________________________________

___________________________________________________________________________

___________________________________________________________________________

___________________________________________________________________________

___________________________________________________________________________

___________________________________________________________________________

2) What would be the elements of a vertical industry Web site for the automotive industry? How could a vertical Web site help Ford Motor Company improve quality?

______________________________________________________________________

______________________________________________________________________

______________________________________________________________________

______________________________________________________________________

______________________________________________________________________

______________________________________________________________________

______________________________________________________________________

______________________________________________________________________

______________________________________________________________________

______________________________________________________________________

### *Assignment 11-C: Case Study: MotivePower, Inc., Railroad Equipment Suppliers*

According to a recent article in the *Wall Street Journal*, longtime industry rivals MotivePower Industries and Westinghouse Air Brake have agreed to merge to create the nation's largest supplier of railroad equipment. MotivePower manufactures and distributes locomotive parts and provides maintenance services, while Westinghouse makes air brakes, compressors, hand brakes, and doors for locomotives and freight cars.[3]

William E. Kassling, chairman and chief executive officer of Westinghouse Air Brake, said,: "The new MotivePower Industries will be uniquely positioned to serve its global customers as a true 'one-stop shop' for a complete package of locomotive and freight car components and services."[4] The creation of the new company provides evidence of the general industry trend to combine services to industry creating tighter vendor and customer relationships. The more businesses know about each other, the better they are able to make improvements in the performance, quality, and costs of their products and services.

In determining the costs associated with a value chain analysis, it is helpful to develop some cost classifications. Structural cost drivers are used to determine activities available to respond to customer needs. Structural cost drivers could include mission and vision,

---

[3] Allana Sullivan and Timothy Aeppel, "MotivePower, Westinghouse Air Brake to Merge in a $633.8 Million Accord," *The Wall Street Journal,* June 4, 1999, p. A6.

[4] "MotivePower Industries and Westinghouse Air Brake Announce Merger of Equals to Create Premier Rail Equipment Supply Company," Westinghouse Air Brake press release, June 4, 1999. Found at http://www.wabco-rail.com/financial/prwabcomotivepower.html on June 9, 1999.

scale, location, technology and complexity. Organizational cost drivers select activities that are used to respond to customer needs. Organizational cost drivers could include total quality management efforts, work force issues, plant layout, and product design implications. Activity cost drivers identify value-added work accomplished to serve customer needs.

- Visit http://www.prnewswire.com/cgi-bin/stories.pl?ACCT=105&STORY=/www/story/06-03-1999/0000954842 for the press release that first talked about the merger with Westinghouse.

1) The creation of an internal value chain depends upon the understanding of cost drivers and how they impact the value chain.[5] Identify potential structural, organizational, and activity cost drivers for MotivePower. Use the air brake product line for your examples.

2) Can a company actually save money by paying more for a component part when comparing two potential vendors? Explain.

[5] See Wayne J. Morse, James R. Davis, Al L. Hartgraves, *Management Accounting, A Strategic Approach*, South-Western College Publishing, Cincinnati, Ohio, 1996, p. 178–179.

3) Westinghouse Air brake has a reputation of using the Japanese manufacturing technique called kaizen, which calls for strict adherence to schedules, procedures, and reductions in cost.[6] How could value chain analysis be used to help achieve the discipline of kaizen?

### *Assignment 11-D: Case Study: Toysmart.com*

Toysmart.com is a small Massachusetts company that aims to be the largest seller on the Internet of intelligent toys for children. The company is counting on a discriminating clientele to buy its collection of safe and sophisticated line of toys. Vendors such as Brio, Playmobil, K'Nex, Alex, and Learning Resources provide the bulk of the products for sale.

Products must meet exacting standards to be accepted for sale by toysmart.com. Product quality tests, play testing, and customer responses are tabulated to determine which items are added and which are dropped from their 20,000-product listing. As such, toysmart.com acts as an agent, filtering out toys that do not meet their standards. Two types of quality control engineers have been hired. Internally, quality control personnel are in charge of customers' online experience. Externally, quality control engineers visit the manufacturing plants of the toy companies, ensuring adherence to internal quality procedures.

The value chain from product inception to payment by the customer is critical to initial customers coming back with repeat sales. Also, toysmart.com is concerned about its reputation in the Internet community for quality and customer service. Sales are expected to climb by word of mouth at a faster rate than by advertising.

[6] Kaizen costing represents efforts to reduce the costs of existing products. Kaizen standards reflect planned improvement for the coming period.

- Visit http://www.toysmart.com for company information and a peek at their extensive toy catalogue.

1) How important is it to toysmart.com to sell quality toys? What is the total cost of a returned product? Remember that this company is just starting business.

2) What business could a toysmart.com engineer have in a Brio plant? How does the quality of the products produced in the valuc chain effect toysmart.com?

3) Customers visiting the Web site want to have a quick and pleasant experience. What possible cost impact would a bad online experience for a customer have on toysmart.com?

4) The need to deliver and bill the correct products on time, usually within 48 hours of the order, is critical to the success of an online business. What modifications to a traditional cost collection system must take place to accommodate this speed?

# Chapter 12

## Quality Costs

The cost of not doing something well is very high in most companies. Rework, scrap, repairs, warranties, schedule delays—all play a part in increasing the cost of doing business. Each of the above cost categories rob company resources, add time to the manufacturing cycle, and disrupt the normal flow of major processes.

For service companies, examples of poor quality are many. Poor quality could result in poor-tasting food, insurance claims that take too much time, an extra long wait in a line for renewal of a driver's license, or a video rental that cannot be played. Service companies with poor quality run the risk of losing customers to competitors.

Successful companies find ways to minimize the costs of poor quality. The first step is to begin active measurements of the costs associated with quality. Prevention costs are incurred to prevent poor quality before it happens. Appraisal costs are incurred while testing products and processes for adherence to specifications and procedures. Internal failure costs result from products and services that do not measure up to specifications or customer needs. External failure costs are incurred when products delivered to customers do not meet customer expectations for performance. Once these costs are measured, management has a basic tool that can be used for both the improvement of product quality and to reduce the cost associated with poor quality.

### *Assignment 12-A: Opening Story: ByCo Insurance Company*

ByCo Insurance Company is a consumer-oriented insurance company focused on life, home, and auto insurance. The company sells all insurance products over the phone. Open 24 hours per day, ByCo provides low prices and high levels of customer service on claims. The business has been growing quickly, especially in rural areas of the country where traditional insurance agents are not easily available.

The concept of quality is relatively new for ByCo. The growth of the company has been driven by adding policyholders as quickly as possible. Once added, however, potential problems may surface. Take, for example, an automobile insurance policy written by an agent who didn't ask enough questions about a prior accident to accurately assess the insurability of a customer. If the result is insuring a customer who turns out to be a bad risk, then the profitability of the company is in jeopardy.

In addition, if customers are sold insurance coverage that is inadequate to cover them from potential risks, they may not get what they think they should get. For example, if a homeowner policy is sold for $150,000 worth of coverage and the actual replacement cost in the event of a loss is $175,000, the customer will have an uninsured loss of $25,000.

Recently, ByCo company executives opened a Web site for direct sales. The initial tests of the site resulted in higher quotes than what live telephone agents have quoted, indicating a conservative bias for the Web site. The executives believe that the Web site will not be successful until the Web site can yield the same results for risk per dollar of insurance coverage as the live agents presently achieve.

1) How are quality costs measured in a service company like ByCo?

2) What is the difference between a manufacturing company and a service company when it comes to the cost of quality?

3) What would be included in ByCo's cost of prevention?

4) From a quality perspective, how should ByCo measure the cost of quality from sales originating from their new Web site?

### *Assignment 12-B: Case Study: Biggie Balloons*

Biggie Balloons is a campus-run business for delivering greetings such as creative balloon designs for all occasions. The balloons can be ordered to commemorate birthdays, passing big exams, or just for fun. The business is based on a large, 20,000-student college campus and has a five-year history.

Traditions have sprung up surrounding the balloon business. Fraternities use balloon-o-grams to notify pledges of acceptance and to announce the receipt of a fraternity pin by a co-ed. The balloon delivery person frequently dresses up for the occasion to enhance the mood of the gift recipient. For example, a birthday balloon gift is likely to be delivered to a dorm room by a person dressed as a clown. An engagement, however, might be delivered by a person wearing a tux.

Arrangements with a local florist have provided a frequently requested new product line—flowers. Flowers can be ordered through Biggie Balloons and delivered either by the florist or by Biggie Balloons. Combinations of both flowers and balloons are also very popular. Management is also looking into delivering singing messages and other unique greeting methods aimed at the college-based customer base.

The following report was recently brought to the attention of the management team by Cindy Starks, quality manager.

**Biggie Balloons**
**Weekly Quality Statistics**
**Week Ending 5/20/2001**

| **Event** | **Frequency** | **Cost** |
|---|---|---|
| Deliveries | 143 | - |
| Broken balloons | 53 | 4.00 |
| Delivery to wrong person | 13 | 238.00 |
| Balloons deflated on way to delivery | 4 | 58.00 |
| View video on proper inflation | 6 | 64.00 |
| Returned bouquet of flowers | 1 | 58.00 |
| Customer complaints | 2 | - |
| Total costs | | 422.00 |

1) Classify the costs in the above chart into preventive and internal failure costs.

2) Are any external failure costs identified? If so, what are they?

3) What is the most significant quality problem? What steps can be taken to reduce the expenditure on this item?

4) What measures can be taken by management to reduce balloon failures?

5) How can customer complaints be significant when they are assigned a zero cost on the report? Can you make any recommendations for improving the weekly quality report?

## *Assignment 12-C: Case Study: H. J. Küpper*

H. J. Küpper is a German manufacturer of precision metal products. The success of the company depends a great deal on the quality of the products they produce. The following information was taken from the H. J. Küpper Web page, located at http://www.kuepper-gruppe.de/english/qualit.htm.[1]

> At H. J. Küpper, Total Quality Management is a central part of corporate strategy. It is achieved by means of integrated quality assurance, backed by CAQ systems,[2] ultramodern measuring equipment and materials laboratories, and documented by certification in line with ISO 9000 and QS 9000.
>
> Together with the customer, the most appropriate solution is devised jointly within the framework of Simultaneous engineering and then turned into reality at Küpper. There are virtually no limits on performance and maximum flexibility is always an outstanding feature.
>
> So too is optimum cost-effectiveness. From test components through to large-volume production, quality is produced systematically and economically, something evidenced by increasing internationalization.

H. J. Küpper's reliance on modern quality techniques is evident from the above. Using ultramodern measuring equipment, the quality system provides assurances that the product will meet all customer requirements. Using international standards such as ISO 9000, H. J. Küpper's products are welcome at companies around the world.

1) What is total quality management? How would H. J. Küpper's use of TQM have an impact on their product's costs?

____________________________________________________________

____________________________________________________________

____________________________________________________________

____________________________________________________________

____________________________________________________________

____________________________________________________________

____________________________________________________________

[1] The Küpper Group, Quality. Author unknown. Taken from http://www.kuepper-gruppe.de/english/qualit.htm on 6/12/99.

[2] A CAQ system is a software program for tracking all aspects of internal quality such as inspection planning, management of inspection orders, inspection data acquisition and evaluation . See http://www.caq.de/english/Products/compact/CompactFrame.htm for more information.

2) H. J. Küpper uses a technique called simultaneous engineering that requires the engineers of both the supplier and the manufacturer to work together on product designs. How does this approach increase quality?

3) How does being ISO 9000 compliant open up international sales possibilities?

## *Assignment 12-D: Team Exercise: Deutsche Motors*

In a project team environment, assign the Deutsche Motors team members the following roles:

- quality assurance manager
- cost accounting manager
- production manager
- engineering manager
- customer representative
- Küpper engineering manager

Note: One or more of the above roles can be combined if team size is limited.

Your team is working for Deutsche Motors, an international company, based in Germany. Deutsche Motors is considering using H. J. Küpper's products for the production of a small, 4-passenger automobile. Conduct a meeting where you will explore how H. J. Küpper's quality system could help Deutsche Motors produce quality automobiles.

**Background:**

- Visit H. J. Küpper's Web site at http://www.kuepper-gruppe.de/english/firma.htm.
- Visit the ISO Web site at http://www.iso.ch/.

**Required:**

- Prepare meeting minutes detailing discussions about H. J. Küpper's quality systems.
- Prepare a group presentation to the board of directors (your class) where each team member highlights findings relative to their particular job function.

# Chapter 13

## Service Company

The need for good cost information is just as important for service companies as it is for manufacturing businesses. Companies in the service industry, such as health care providers, hospitals, financial institutions, insurance companies, and transportation companies, as well as professional organizations all have a tremendous stake in accurate cost information. The system used must deliver accurate information to arrive at correct pricing decisions, especially when service companies face stiff competition.

Service industry companies have recently turned to activity-based management and activity-based costing to provide them with strategic, operational, and financial information.[1] Many service firms sell products on a fixed-contract basis prior to knowing what the actual costs are going to be. With good tracking of the activities that drive costs, these companies can make timely decisions on potential issues that affect profitability.

### *Assignment 13-A: Opening Story: Green Cross Insurance Company*

Green Cross Insurance Company provides health care for a small community in upstate New York. The company has grown steadily over the last few years by offering reasonably priced services combined with a large network of participating doctors and physicians. The most popular option is Green HMO, which combines low prices with primary physician-directed care. Customers who elect Green HMO select a doctor who oversees care and a co-payment plan that discourages unnecessary trips to the doctor.

Green Cross has competition in the HMO market. Competitors go directly to area employers and propose plans for their employees at either lower prices for the same services or increased services for about the same price. Either way, Green Cross needs to be able to predict their costs in order to compete successfully.

Rival White Mountain Care has just introduced a new HMO package to the people at Northern Forestry. Northern Forestry employs 1,500 persons in the region and is the largest employer. Northern Forestry permits employees to choose various health plans once per calendar year. The package offered will cost the average employee $3.85 per week less than the Green HMO plan presently in place. Although the plan offers one or two features less than the Green HMO plan, employees usually vote for health plans that will save them tangible amounts of money.
Green HMO director of sales, Janice Jones, is worried. She knows from experience that employees often jump at the lowest cost proposal and is wondering if she should match

---

[1] Steve Player and Carol Cobble, *Cornerstones of Decision Making: Profiles of Enterprise ABM*, Oakhill Press, Greensboro, NC, 1999.

the $3.85 per week price reduction. Gunther Weaver, the new manager of cost management, is not very optimistic. In a recent meeting, Gunther stated, "Janice, the latest cost report indicates that the service we give to Northern Forest employees is correctly priced. Although the system uses traditional methods for allocating administrative costs, I'm convinced that we are achieving our goal of a 15 percent return on this contract." "I'm not so sure, Gunther." Janice continued, "I work this account on a daily basis, and I know from experience that it takes far less of my time than accounts half its size. Northern Forest has a great human resources department and they handle 95 percent of the questions and even work directly with some of the doctors. We should be making way more than 15 percent on this account."

1) How could the concept of activity-based costing be applied to a service business like Green Cross?

2) Green Cross's president recently said that all systems in the company need to be re-aligned to take advantage of strategic opportunities. How does making changes in the cost system help the company take advantage of opportunities?

3) What opportunities do you see for Green Cross to reevaluate the cost system?

4) Could customer profitability be improved with the installation of an activity-based costing system at Green Cross? Explain.

### *Assignment 13-B: Case Study: Providence Mutual Fund*

The new product development team at Providence Mutual Fund has spent the last three months taking a long look at the cost of managing the growth sector funds of the company. The company charges a flat 1.5 percent management fee on all assets managed. The fee is calculated based on the total dollar value of assets in the fund on a certain day, and charged to accounts twice per year. Although the fee is high enough to cover expenses and contribute to profit, recent stock market performance and customer withdrawals have dropped the asset base 20 percent below the prior period.

Fund managers feel that the stock market downturn and the recent customer withdrawals of money from the fund are temporary occurrences. The board of directors of the company has other ideas. In order to preserve the profitability of the company, the board has requested a full analysis of all costs associated with running the fund. A team of individuals, including stockbrokers, administrative help, computer specialists, and activity cost consultants, has been gathered by the firm to comply with the board's request.

The first area of concern found by the group is administrative fees. The group found that the growth sector administrative fees were $256,219 over budget, well above the amount allocated to cover such expenses. An activity vs. budget report established by the group produced the following results.

**Providence Mutual Fund**
**Monthly Activity Report - Growth Sector**
**Month Ending December, 2001**

| Activity | Monthly Activity | Budget | Cost | Bud-Cost |
|---|---|---|---|---|
| Processing new accounts | 345 | 32,000 | 20,650 | 11,350 |
| Mailing prospectuses | 933 | 12,000 | 10,350 | 1,650 |
| Processing monthly stock rpts. | 24,352 | 2,200,000 | 2,191,680 | 8,320 |
| Filing SEC registration materials | 9 | 12,000 | 15,687 | (3,687) |
| Training | 14 | 9,000 | 10,200 | (1,200) |
| Phone requests | 4,860 | 378,000 | 437,400 | (59,400) |
| Personal/sick/vacation time | 45 | 125,000 | 129,600 | (4,600) |
| Closing old accounts | 8,565 | 150,000 | 342,600 | (192,600) |
| Mailing checks | 9,388 | 21,500 | 37,552 | (16,052) |
| | | 2,939,500 | 3,195,719 | (256,219) |

1) How can looking at the activities that generate the administrative costs help Providence Mutual Fund control costs? Give examples.

2) The closing old accounts activity generated the highest budget variance. Is this the major problem area for Providence Mutual Fund? Why or why not?

3) What can be said about value-added and non-value-added costs given in the report? List any assumptions you need to make to develop your answer.

4) Which activities should be targets for cost reduction? why?

### Team Exercises

5) Go to www.google.com and look up activity-based management. Find information about relating the concept of ABM to the service industry.

6) Go to http://www.rpm-abm.com/faq.htm and look for the definition of non-value-added activities. Prepare a report based upon Providence Mutual Fund on how the definition for non-value-added activities could be used to help examine costs at Providence Mutual Fund.

7) Prepare a management report and present to the class the team's plan of action for reducing the administrative costs for Providence Mutual Fund.

## *Assignment 13-C: Case Study: DiscJockey.com*

DiscJockey.com is the third-leading purveyor of music over the Internet.[2] The business centers on broadcasting radio signals over the Internet. With over 100 channels of music to choose from, listeners are always pleased with the selections. The music selections play without the DJ chatter found on over-the-air stations and with very limited commercials. Listeners can even request music from online play lists. E-mail notification is sent directly to requestors when their selection is going to be played.

[2] Dyke Hendrickson, DiscJockey.com has Investors Humming Their Tune, *Mass High Tech,* MassTech Communications, Volume 17, issue 17 April 26–May 2, 1999, p. 5.

DiscJockey.com started as a simple way to advertise a record-spinning DJ business; owner Richard Chadwick now has six full-time and several dozen part-time employees. Each musical selection is placed into digital form, then programmed into several computers for replay over the Internet. Customers are required to have a free streaming audio player installed on their PCs in order to play the music.

Recently, several investors have approached Chadwick about either buying his business or providing him with investment money for expansions. In order to properly prepare for the visits, Mr. Chadwick needs good cost information. The business of producing streaming audio for broadcast over the Internet depends primarily on having the computing power to handle thousands of simultaneous connections. Additionally, the computers need high-performance connections to the Internet. Most of the activity that drives costs will come from Internet users requesting the music channels the company will provide.

The consultant suggested that the major activities of the operation be looked at to determine

- the outputs of the process
- the customer for the output
- the quality measurement for the output
- the activities required to produce the output
- the resources consumed by the activities
- how the activities add value, and the cost drivers of the activities

1) Activity-based costing is being proposed by a consultant for DiscJockey.com. How could ABC help DiscJockey.com get a handle on its costs?

2) Using the consultant's list above, determine how DiscJockey.com should answer each question posed.

3) Explain how the answers to Question 2 will help DiscJockey.com determine how the investor's money should be spent.

# Appendix A

## Teamwork

### *The Importance of Teamwork*

Businesses across the country are using teams and teamwork more and more today. A recent survey (1997 WorkUSA Survey by Watson Wyatt Worldwide) indicated that over half of the 9,144 employees surveyed worked on teams.[1] Today, teams are growing not only in numbers but also in the importance of the tasks that management is assigning to them. Customer service teams, product introduction teams, cost reduction teams, and continuous improvement teams, just to name a few, are forming on a daily basis.

Teams give companies the potential to tap the mind power of all team members acting with a singular focus. With the collaborative power of people with complementary skills working on the same goal, amazing things can happen. High levels of energy, focus, and directive purpose can flow from teams if they are properly established, directed, and supported.

Contrasting with a well-run team, however, is the potential for a team to function at a level that is lower than what individuals can achieve on their own. A dysfunctional team, or one that just is not working, can be very disruptive to a company and upsetting to employees.

Students experience teamwork in the class project teams they are assigned to and in teams organized by the service or academic organizations they join. This chapter will focus on using teamwork on project teams.

**Defining a Team**

What is a team? According to Katzenbach and Smith, "A team is a small number of people with complementary skills who are committed to a common purpose, performance goals, and approach for which they hold themselves mutually accountable."[2] Glenn Parker generally agrees, calling a team "a group of people with a high degree of inter-dependence geared toward the achieving of a goal or the completion of a task."[3]

Student project teams share similar characteristics to the team definitions given. Project teams made up of classmates from a particular course share a common purpose, have performance goals, and normally are mutually accountable for results. The level of inter-

---

[1] WorkUSA Web site: http://www.watsonwyatt.com, visited 2/9/99.
[2] Katzenbach and Smith, *The Wisdom of Teams,* McKinsey & Company, Inc., New York, 1993, p. 45.
[3] Parker, Glenn, *Cross-Functional Teams: Working with Allies, Enemies and other Strangers*, Jossy-Bass Publishers, San Francisco, 1994, p. 35.

dependence in achieving a goal will depend on how the project responsibilities are presented to the team.

**The Beginning of a Team**

Companies that begin teams should take care to give the new team a good start. New and ongoing teams need to be built on a strong foundation. The foundation should consist of the following:

1. A common goal or purpose
2. Adequate team skills or resources to accomplish the goal
3. Good direction and support from the sponsor
4. Clear schedule, due dates, and deliverables
5. Clear team performance measurements

The common goal or purpose is an essential requirement. A group cannot function as a team unless every member of the team knows what they need to do to accomplish the team's goal. Well-coordinated efforts help smooth the way for member's contributions to be added to the group's effort at just the right time. A unified purpose helps members determine what effort is needed and when to move the team closer to task completion.

The team members and the skills they bring to the team can be the difference in accomplishing a goal or falling short. A team tackling a product improvement needs input from product designers, assemblers, and testers. They also need input from management accountants who can calculate the cost implication to the team's suggested changes. The team also needs to be able to recognize and take decisive action when it needs additional resources from outside the team in order to finish a task.

Getting good direction and support from the sponsor of the team can also make or break a team's performance. Teams without a solid focus will tend to drift off on side issues and rarely get anything substantial accomplished. Good direction is like a roadmap. Good maps allow you to plan, conserve resources, and arrive at your destination in an efficient manor.

A team's sponsor is the person or organization that initially pulled the team together. In a company setting it could be a department or functional group head. In a student team situation, the sponsor is normally a course instructor or group advisor. Weak support from the team's sponsor adds confusion and uncertainty to the team situation. A few of the symptoms of weak support include the sponsor not being available to the group for questions and possible confusion between how the sponsor will measure the group's performance. Any lack of strong direction coming from the sponsor can have a negative effect on team performance.

A clear schedule, due dates, and deliverables are required for good team focus. Each team member should be fully aware of the deadlines facing the group and what his or her contributions are supposed to be. Due dates should be established early in the team meeting process and reviewed at every team meeting. Unrealistic dates should be revised and new targets set. The team also has a responsibility to notify the person or the organization expecting results if the delay will cause the team to miss a deadline. Team performance measurements often dictate how well a team functions. If members feel that their individual contributions will either not be valued or are not needed, those team members have a tendency to withdraw their efforts from the team. Instructors need to have a clear method in place for ensuring participation from all team members or some students could give less than their best effort. For example, student teams where one person becomes the dominant member have a tendency to leave most of the project work to that individual.

In work situations, the lack of team performance measures could result in people giving minimal efforts to the team. For example, a management accountant assigned to a cost reduction team is getting mixed signals from her boss. When she is away from her normal work area performing team business, she receives a pile of questions and additional work from her boss. Clearly, this management accountant will not give freely of her time to help move the team forward as long as she feels her boss does not approve. If, however, the boss included her team performance in her performance review and was clearly supportive of her team efforts, her participation on the team would most likely improve.

**Roles on a Team**

Once an individual joins a team, that individual will be asked to perform various roles that help a team function. Some of these roles include the following:

- Individual contributor
- Leader
- Facilitator
- Recorder
- Liaison

The individual contributor has probably the most important role of all on a team. Individual contributors take the actions that lead to the completion of team goals. A good individual contributor helps keep the team focused on the task at hand. Each person on the team has the responsibility to help keep the project moving forward, meet team commitments, and help other group members.

The team leader has a difficult but rewarding job. It is the responsibility of the team leader to ensure that the team has the resources it needs and that all members are committed to the team goals and the commitments they have made to the team. In addition, the team leader is usually responsible for ensuring that the final product does indeed meet or exceed what the team committed to accomplish.

A facilitator is a person either inside or from outside the team who is responsible for keeping the team's processes functioning. One such process could be a team meeting. If the team begins to stray from the purpose of the meeting, the facilitator will help bring the team back on track. A facilitator could also be helpful in resolving any team conflicts with project direction or with personalities. Every team member carries team facilitation responsibilities.

The team recorder is responsible for recording team commitments and progress toward making those commitments happen. Minutes[4] of meetings, scheduling of meetings, and co-ordination of work between team members are just a few of the possible job activities for the team recorder. This position is usually shared by all team members.

A liaison is a person who serves as a connection from the team to the person or group that is looking for the group's output. For a student team, the liaison could be a team member who visits frequently with the professor who assigned the team project. This critical role is essential in getting results that not only meet what the team set out accomplish, but also meet the needs of the customer of the output.

**Team Members**

Are you a good team member? Do you know what you will need to do to contribute to your team at the highest level? Participation on teams is seldom an option. More and more, businesses and organizations are using teams to get work done. Yet everyone is supposed to automatically know how to be a good team member. A team effort will often fail because the individual members of a team fail to meet some very basic levels of performance.

According to Glenn Parker, teamwork consultant and author of several books on teamwork,[5] a team member competency profile include the following:

1. Keep other members informed and up to date on team issues.
2. Participate willingly in most team activities.
3. Express positive expectations of other team members in terms of their abilities and contributions.
4. Publicly credit the input and expertise of other team members.
5. Genuinely value the input and expertise of other team members.
6. Bring conflicts within the team into the open in an effort to resolve them.
7. Speak of teammates in positive terms.

---

[4] Minutes are careful notes of team meetings that can be used by the team as a reference.

[5] Glenn Parker's books include *Cross-Functional Teams: Working With Allies, Enemies and Other Strangers, Best Practices for Teams, Volume 1, Best Practices for Teams, Volume 2, Team Players and Teamwork.* More information can be found at http://www.glennparker.com. List of team member competencies posted to Teamnet listserv (teamnet-l V1 #1244, teamnet-l@davinci.cascss.unt.edu) on April 16, 1999. Used with permission.

8. Promote a friendly climate among team members.
9. Keep other members informed and up to date regarding actions and events that may influence the team.
10. Be a good team player.
11. Praise and recognize teammates in other ways for their work.
12. Encourage and support the contributions of teammates.
13. Willing to learn from others on the team.
14. Do fair share of the work required by the team.
15. Show respect for the intelligence of teammates.
16. Encourage and help organize team get-togethers that promote team spirit.
17. Share all relevant or useful information with teammates.
18. Protect and defend the team's reputation with key people outside of the team.
19. Empower teammates or encourage them to act as if they are empowered to take actions that support the team's goals.
20. Solicit ideas and opinions from others to help the team reach a decision or develop a plan.
21. Support and, where appropriate, work to implement team decisions.
22. Speak positively about teammates to key stakeholders outside of the team.
23. Help teammates feel and act as if their contributions are important.
24. Share freely all knowledge, skills, and expertise.
25. Seek the involvement of members in all aspects of the team's process.
26. Promote the work of the team with outsiders.
27. Help develop an informal, relaxed climate that makes the team a fun setting for work.

The best list of team member responsibilities is a list that the team itself makes up and agrees to, thus it may be best to start with blank paper and have teams brainstorm a list of responsibilities. However, the previous list is available if necessary.

**Meeting Management**

Meetings are a mainstay of communication and getting things done in modern organizations. Keeping many people up to date on matters that affect the department, the team, and the business occurs on a continual basis. The major types of meetings are

- Informational
- Problem solving
- Task updating

The purpose of informational meetings is to get a consistent message delivered to all meeting participants. As an individual participant in this type of meeting, your objective should be to listen carefully and to ask questions that will clarify any questions you may have about the message. Informational meetings work well when a number of people need to be updated right away on an issue.

Problem-solving meetings are highly participatory. This is when team members get to brainstorm new approaches, discuss issues that could impact on team performance, and gain consensus on how the team will proceed on the issues at hand.

Task-updating meetings are for teams that have their team's work well underway. The purpose of the meeting is to get a status report from all team members and to analyze any potential problems. If the team feels that any commitments made by the team will not be met, the team will explore the options they may have to either get more resources or to re-schedule commitments.

**The Meeting Agenda**

The agenda is an extremely important meeting management tool. The agenda lays out the topics for discussion, identifies who is responsible for each topic, and lays out the meeting time set aside for each item. Here's an example of a typical meeting agenda:

Accounting Project Team Meeting Agenda

Start Time: 7 PM Where: Library Meeting Room 7a
End Time: 9 PM

Who: Members of the Accounting Project Team, Accounting 205

| Topics | Responsible | Time allotted: |
|---|---|---|
| Minutes of last meeting | Jerry T. | 5 minutes |
| Financial statements | Sherry B./Joan C. | 30 minutes |
| Project narrative | Cathy B. | 15 minutes |
| Audio/visual preparations | Tim M. | 20 minutes |
| Web Site design and launch | Sheila B. | 30 minutes |
| Team progress assessment | All team members | 10 minutes |
| Meeting feedback and next agenda | All team members | 10 minutes |

Notice that every minute of the meeting time is accounted for. Team members can adjust the time allocated to each topic during the meeting if each member agrees. Teams that are working well will agree ahead of time on how much flexibility they will permit. Too much flexibility will cause the team to look upon the agenda as a worthless activity; too little flexibility will render the agenda a straightjacket. Good teams will find a balance that creates the best working environment for their situation.

## Using Business Project Teams

Using a capital expenditure as an example, a project team is normally formed for the purpose of providing an analysis of project expenditures, presentation of the project proposal to management and, possibly, to work on the project implementation teams.

At each stage of the process, close teamwork is required. Project teams need good and consistent direction from the management team with frequent feedback sessions on progress. Communication within the team is critical to keep the project on track. Teams that hold meetings on a regular basis to evaluate progress tend to stay on track. Continual assessment of areas where the team needs outside help, additional resources, or simply more output from team members will keep the team motivated and informed.

The process of getting a team involved in the decision helps the eventual outcome of the capital project in several ways. First, if the team is properly composed, they will be made up of people who will not only be directly involved in the project but also be directly affected by the outcome of the project. This up-front involvement ensures no surprises once the project is completed. The department that will have the direct responsibility to implement the project will have first-hand knowledge of how the new capital is supposed to work. This will help establish a commitment to achieving the project's financial and performance goals.

Within the team, individual commitment to achieving project outcomes is critical. If all team members are singing the same song from the same sheet of music, the project will run smoothly. If, however, individual members start acting in their own self-interest, the project performance is sure to suffer. Good leadership within the team and strong support from the organization or office to which the team reports will help ensure that the objectives of the team are met.

Student projects also need strong direction and good leadership. Teams need to develop a game plan early on that identifies the roles each student will play and details a time line for performance. Often student projects reach the last hour prior to a deadline and a critical resource such as a printer or a color copier is unavailable. Quality of the effort definitely suffers when your options for adding extras such as schedules and first-class presentation techniques take a back shelf to simply getting the basic job done on time.

## Exercises

Team warm-up exercises:

1. Have each team member write down his/her answer to the question, "What are the characteristics of a great project team?" Each individual will then introduce him/herself and give his or her answer to the question. All answers should be recorded. When everyone is finished, the team should compile a condensed list to be used as a guideline for team performance.

2. Each team member is asked to record his or her impressions about what made a team that they have been a member of great. This could be a sports team, a high-school project team, or a civic group such as scouting. Once recorded, the team should list common elements from each experience.

First meeting guidelines:

1. At the first team meeting, teams need to decide who will be the project leader and recorder, and begin a discussion about the task at hand.

2. All needed information should be brought to the meeting, such as project documentation, sample reports, instructor handouts, etc.

3. Team rules, guidelines, and acceptable behavior should be established early. For example, the consequences for missing a team meeting should be identified at the first meeting.

4. All team members should be prepared to discuss what they can contribute to the team and be ready to make firm commitments to getting the job done.

5. All agreements should be placed into the team minutes and distributed at the next meeting.

# Appendix B

## Internet Skills

The Internet. Just a few short years ago, the Internet was funded by the government and run by large academic institutions. E-mail was a mysterious method of keeping up with research projects by professors at Stamford and MIT. Modems moved data at very slow speeds (by comparison to today). A few businesses such as Prodigy and The Well sprung up to distribute e-mail, but the business world generally ignored the whole development. Businesses continued to ignore the Internet until the invention of the World Wide Web and the tool that made it simple, the browser.

In 1993, the Internet was not well known outside of academic circles. Large companies began adding e-mail to their local networks. From its humble beginnings to the economic force of today, the Internet has changed the way people and businesses communicate.[1] It is not only here today but it has changed the skills needed to do almost every job.

The skills needed today by business professionals, including management accountants, are as follows:

1. Researching, locating, and validating information both online and in systems
2. Communicating electronically offline
3. Communicating online
4. Transmitting data over networks
5. Working remotely
6. Integrating existing systems with the network
7. Empowering information users

For further discussion on the origins of the Internet, visit *The Business of the Internet* online companion, chapter one, http://course.com/downloads/mis/biznet/chapter1.html.

### *Researching on the Internet*

Finding good information on the Internet is a challenge. While no one can say exactly, it is certain that the number of unique Web pages on the Internet today is well over 100 million and growing. Finding good, accurate information that can be used for business decisions is a challenge for even the most seasoned Internet explorer.

Four methods are commonly used to find information on the Internet. These methods are using search engines, developing your bookmark or favorites file, visiting trusted Web sites, and keeping your eyes and ears open for new Web sites. The best Internet researchers will use a combination of all four methods.

---

[1] See *How the Web is Different from Other Media*, located at http://www.davewolin.com/webdiff.htm, for an explanation of how the Internet has changed the way we communicate.

## *Using Search Engines*

Search engines are the most commonly used method of finding information on the Internet. Unfortunately, they are commonly the cause of the most frustration and the fewest quality results. The reasons are fairly simple. Search engines have several limitations every researcher should be aware of. First of all, search engines lack intelligence. They can search only for keywords inputted by you. They cannot look beyond the keyword or relate to why you are asking for the information or what it could possibly mean.

Secondly, search engines are only as good as the programs they send out to the computers connected to the Internet to collect Web page information. According to http://searchenginewatch.com, each major search engine sends "spiders" or "crawlers" into the Internet on a continuous basis, looking for new information. The efficiency of the data collections will affect the ability of the search engine to produce results. Searchenginewatch.com tracks all major search engines and records how often and how much data is collected.

The third major factor that separates the performance of search engines is how efficient the search engine is in matching information requested from searchers to information contained in their databases. Remember, you are not searching the Internet. You are searching what the "spiders" have found and filed into a database. In essence, you are relying on the ability of the search engine to locate the information you want from the search engine's internal database.

If you are going to use a major search engine such as Alta Vista, Excite, HotBot, Lycos, or Infoseek to look for business information, the most important thing to do first is to think about what you want the end product to be. In other words, if you found the information you were seeking, what would it look like? What key words would appear in the Web page? Are those key words unique to your search? If so, the major search engines will most likely yield multiple hits, or returns of Web pages, with the information you seek. If the words you use are very common, the pages returned by a search engine are likely to cover many off-topic subjects.

## *Using a Trusted Source*

If you know the address of an Internet site that consistently provides accurate and timely information, then you do not need a search engine to find what you want on the Internet. The method most often used by professionals is to find a trusted source on the Internet. Trusted accounting sites that typically rank high among financial professionals include the following:

- AICPA Web Site http://www.aicpa.org
- Rutgers Accounting Web http://www.rutgers.edu/Accounting
- Accounting Net http://accountingnet.com

These sites are monitored by professionals, continually updated and expanded upon, and have easy site navigation and internal searching capabilities. Your first stop for financial information on the Internet should be one of these Web sites.

For information on stocks, bonds, mutual funds, and company performance, look to Dailystocks.com. Dailystocks.com, a part of the FinancialWeb.com family of Web sites, is a financial resource for all professionals and can be used as a one-stop center for all relevant information about any publicly traded U.S. company. Stock quotes, charts, five-year financial information, EDGAR reporting, and much more data are available.

### *Using a Meta-Search Engine*

Meta-search engines are search engines that take your keywords and search several major search engines at the same time. This is very useful because not all search engines are built the same.

Here's how they work. First, a user must go to the Web site of the meta-search engine and enter a search criteria, usually a keyword. A keyword is a word or short phrase that has a very high probability of being found in a Web page. The program then sends your request to as many as ten search engines, such as AltaVista, Excite, Web Crawler, Info Seek, GoTo.com, Northern Lights, and HotBot.

Once the request gets to these search engines, each individual search will have a very limited amount of time, usually from 30 to 60 seconds, to find the requested information. Results are then returned to your browser in the order that the individual search engines found the information. This means that the first few returned Web sites are not necessarily the best fits for your search criteria. The user must look through the entire list to determine the best Web sites to actually visit.

The meta-search engines will return summary information to your browser. The user then selects the sites to be visited. Clicking on the selected sites brings the user to the requested information.

### *Creating a Web Page*

The creation of a Web page opens up an avenue of communication that was unavailable to business professionals a few years ago. The ability to electronically send text and graphics simultaneously to dozens or thousands of people at the same time sets Web pages apart from other means of sharing data. Companies will be posting information on internal Web sites and sharing information with customers via Web pages at an ever increasing pace. The reasons are simple. The medium is low in cost and represents a very high level of speed. Learning about how Web pages work is an essential part of the modern professional toolkit.

Creating a Web page can be a simple task. The basic language used to create Web pages, HTML, is very easy to understand and work with. HTML, or hyper-text markup language, was created in 1992 as a way of marking up documents so that computers using browsers could read them. The reason you should learn something about HTML is the same reason that we teach kids multiplication tables before we let them use calculators. It's helpful to have a basic understanding of HTML before you rely on a program to do it for you so that you can resolve any problems you may encounter along the way.

Fortunately, many free sources are available to help you learn the basics of HTML. Some of the best are

- Hotwired Web Monkey, at http://www.hotwired.com/webmonkey
- HTML Goodies at http://www.htmlgoodies.com
- Builder.com's HTML for beginners at http://builder.cnet.com/Authoring/Basics/
- NCSA-A Beginner's Guide to HTML at http://www.ncsa.uiuc.edu/General/Internet/WWW/HTMLPrimer.html

Once you know the basics, there are some excellent free programs available to create your own Web pages. The most common program is Netscape's Composer. Composer comes free when you download the full version of the Netscape Navigator browser. Composer is a "what you see is what you get" program. In other words, you can load text and graphics into composer and the HTML code will be generated automatically. At the simplest level, a Web page creator could take a file from a word processing program and use the cut and paste function to lay the text into composer. Composer then creates the HTML needed for a browser to display the file.

Other HTML authoring software programs are available for just about any price range and can be found at http://download.com or at http://www.tucows.com.

### *Getting Data from a Database*

The Internet started as a network for interrupted communications between research universities and for the military.[2] When companies caught on to the idea of networking computers both inside and outside the company, Internet technologies were called upon to move information. Companies soon found out, however, that getting computers to communicate and share files was just the start of a communications revolution. What they needed next was to have quick and secure access to the wealth of information they have been storing in databases for years.

---

[2] See Neal J. Hannon, *The Business of the Internet,* Course Technology, 1998, pp. 10–11.

Why would a company need to tap into a database from any computer connected to the network? Consider the information a company carries in a large database. It could include detailed sales history, customer complaints, quality reports on individual products, production schedules, and vender information. Traditionally, employees who needed this information to answer a question or to prepare a forecast, etc., needed to load the database program and run a report. This report would then have to be analyzed and modified for the particular purpose. This is time consuming and costly.

Databases that are accessible on the company's network promise quick access to information. The data is also ready to place directly into other desktop tools, such as spreadsheets, for analysis. Additionally, information that is available on a desktop computer gives the employee the ability to answer questions as soon as they come in, increasing the speed of business.

There are two basic methods of extracting information from large databases. The first method is to Web-enable the database itself. Web-enabling a database means making the information inside the database accessible to individuals who have authorized access to the company's internal data network. Large database software companies such as Oracle and Sybase include this feature in a majority of the new products they sell today.

The second way to open access to database information is to use new software tools called middleware. Middleware acts as the go-between from computers on the network and the large databases. Recently, companies focused exclusively on creating middleware for the unlocking of databases have found a large market for their services. Companies are opening up their databases using middleware, creating an increased worker productivity.

### *Creating Secure Passwords*

Security of information in a business network is everyone's job. As companies move to make more managerial accounting information available to employees and customers, the need to keep the information secure increases. Security starts with the users of the system.

Users are given access to a system by the issuance of user identification (user ID) and password. The initial user ID and password is usually a simple combination of the user's name and a short, easy to remember phrase. The user should change this short phrase after the first time the user enters the system. That is when the first security problems could occur. If the user never changes his or her initial password, other users or outsiders could easily guess the access to the system. Good password procedures and controls can help to prevent security problems.

System security starts with a company's security policy. The policy will state what the company wants to protect and why. The policy will also specify who should have access to the various files and systems in the network and who should not have access. Good password control helps companies to ensure that no unauthorized access occurs.

A good password is a password that is easy for the person using the password to remember but very difficult for someone else to guess. Common words found in a dictionary are the least secure passwords. Pet names, names of children, etc., do not make good passwords. The most common word used for a password is the word *password* itself. A poor password is any password that is easy to guess.

Good passwords are passwords that are uncommon, even meaningless to everyone but the owner of the password. Systems that allow for lower case and upper case letters and numbers offer an increased chance for secure passwords. For example, if a person were to take three very common things and combine them in a unique way, the outcome would be a secure password.

- your brother's little league team: The Astro's
- your father's date of birth: 7-3-55
- your graduation date: 5-20-03

Combined together, your password becomes: "A7355st52003ro", which is a password that has meaning only to you. You could shorten the password to "As5503tro" or "03Ast7355." The point is to create a password that is meaningful to you but nearly impossible for others to guess.

**Password Exercises:**

1. Why is a secure password critical to system security?
2. Create a secure password from common phrases and numbers.
3. Why is system security important to management accounting?
4. Your password should never be given to someone else. True or false? Explain.

**Search Engine Exercises:**

1) Go to http://searchenginewatch.com/facts/math.html and look up the information on search engine math. Construct a search for standard and job-order costs using math symbols as displayed on the Web page.

________________________________________

________________________________________

________________________________________

________________________________________

________________________________________

2) Document your results as to how Alta Vista, Excite, and HotBot use symbols to help users add and subtract information from searches. Write a short report on the search findings.

3) Provide three reasons why the ranking in Alta Vista is different from the rankings in Excite. Hint: Searchenginewatch.com will have information on how each search engine ranks pages for your searches.

## Finding Financial Information: Amazon.com

1) Use http://dailystocks.com to find Amazon.Com, Inc. Once at the dailystocks.com site, enter the ticker symbol "amzn" and click on the five-year income statement. For the year ending December 31, 1998, by how much did general and administrative expenses exceed gross profit? Can the company continue to have general and administrative expenses exceed gross profit? Explain your answer.

2) Go to the Dell computer site at http://www.dell.com and find a package price for a desktop Pentium III computer with a 550 MHz clock speed, with everything included. Be sure to list all elements of the package price. Next, go to http://www.onsale.com and find the price for a comparable system. Be sure to document your system comparisons to insure that you are pricing a comparable system. Write a 200-word report documenting your findings. Include in your report your assessment of using the Internet as a tool for lowering the cost of doing business.

## Using Search Engines

1) Go to www.dogpile.com and use the Web site to look up the words "activity-based costing." Look for a description of how an actual ABC software package works and write a 200-word report on your findings. Outline your report below.

2) Compare the results from two major search engines within dogpile.com. What were the first five sites found in Yahoo? What were the first five sites found in GoTo.com? Why are they different? How far into the results did you have to go to find relevant information?

3) Write a 200-word paper on the advantages and disadvantages to using a meta-search engine over a single search engine. Be sure to include information you discovered when searching for "activity-based costing." Outline your report below.

4) Use a meta-search engine to find an article on how a company is using ABC costing to improve its business. Summarize the article in a 150-word report. Outline your report below.

**Using Databases**:

1) Go to http://www.oracle.com/businessonline/ and check out how a company such as Oracle makes information from databases available through standard Web browsers. Write a 200-word report on how this product works and what promise it holds for companies looking to speed business transactions. Outline your report below.

2) Go to http://www.sybase.com/industry_solutions/ and find a solution for an industry group such as financial services, heath care, or telecommunications. How does Sybase provide secure Web-based transactions for your chosen industry group?

**Creating Web Pages: Possible Focus Areas**

1. Annual budgeting process project
2. Posting monthly financial information Web page
3. Creating a team-based Web page
4. Project team Web page
5. Suppliers information Web page
6. Using bulletin boards and discussion groups for managerial accounting information
7. Not-for-profit informational Web page for Habitat for Humanity
8. Strategic performance Web page
9. Non-financial indicators Web page (training, customer complaints, field failures)
10. Customer service/ total product costs Web page

# Appendix C

## Communication and Analytical Skills

The ability to communicate has the potential to set a person apart from the crowd. The communication of thoughts, ideas, and actions is the core essence of getting things done. Great communicators provide a clear vision that others can easily follow. Business collaboration, or getting things done with the help of others, requires that all parties have a clear understanding of exactly what needs to be accomplished. That idea can be communicated electronically, in writing, or face to face.

### *Effective E-mail*

Dr. Norman Vincent Peale said in 1983, "To be able to communicate effectively not only with an audience, but one to one, goes far toward determining our own success in life." [1] Still true today, the ability to effectively communicate often decides what gets done and who does it as well. A well-articulated plan often serves as the basis for managerial action. Effective communication includes oral and written communication. In some organizations, the ability to effectively communicate using electronic means is extremely important. Effective electronic communication is the ability to express ideas and opinions using means such as voice mail, e-mail, and desktop videoconferencing. In addition, effective electronic communication also includes the ability to gather appropriate information from internal and external online networks and create meaningful presentations from that information.

E-mail permits users to communicate even if the other party is not physically present at the time the communication is attempted. This means that communication can happen at any time of the day or night. Marion Weiler, writing in a recent edition of *Messaging Magazine,* talks about how people at the major oil company Chevron use e-mail to exchange information.

> It (e-mail) provided the ability for people and applications to communicate electronically from their desktops asynchronously rather than synchronously as with telephones—eliminating phone tag. It allowed the exchange of detailed and easily revisable information. It meant that the delays in communication cycle times were the result of how quickly people could get to and process information, rather than being the result of delays in the manual delivery of the medium itself as is the case with traditional mail and fax.[2]

Quicker exchanges of information, coupled with a detailed record of the communication, have helped to improve the speed at which business is conducted.

---

[1] P. Swets, *The Art of Talking So That People Will Listen,* Prentice Hall Press, 1983: p. xi.

[2] Marion Weiler, "Chevron Perspectives on Messaging", *Messaging Magazine,* found at http://www.ema.org/html/pubs/mmv3n1/chevron.htm, 2/23/99.

E-mail provides the ability for people and computers to communicate from desktop to desktop, even when they are not at their computers. Telephones require both parties to be present for meaningful communication to take place.

E-mail, according to a recent *Business Week* article quoting Forrester Research, is expected to reach over 12 billion messages by the end of 2001.[3] Businesses are relying on e-mail to communicate both within the company and to customers. Clearly, good e-mail writing skills and techniques are a major part of everyday business communications.

A well-constructed e-mail message should follow a few simple guidelines. First, the subject line of the e-mail should be compelling. The object here is to get the reader to open the e-mail message. This is important because the average businessperson can receive hundreds of e-mail messages per week. Your message is competing with all other e-mail messages for the time and attention of the reader, therefore it is important to convey to the reader a reason for viewing your e-mail. For example, a strong subject line such as "Need Approval for Expenditure" would be better than "Office Supplies." "Budget Meeting with Sales on 10/2/2000" would be preferred to "Budget Meeting."

The e-mail message itself should be brief, clear, and to the point.[4] The message creates an electronic file that can be received and acted upon immediately or responded to later. Short messages that either give specific information or request a specific action are best. Try to anticipate and answer all your recipient's potential questions. This will help to prevent several rounds of e-mail messages.

The technique you use for answering a message is another way to improve your e-mail communications. Most software e-mail packages will permit you to arrange your reply messages around the statements or questions from the original message. In Figure C-1, the original message is presented with > signs in front of the first e-mail message.

---

[3] *Business Week Online*, July 13, 1998. Report by Patrick Lambert—staff reporter

[4] N. Hannon, "The Business of the Internet" *Course Technology, Inc., 1998,* p. 58.

***Figure C-1***

From: yorkteam@yorkteam.com
To: <nhannon@tiac.net>
Subject: Permission to Link and Use Information
Date: Fri, 12 Feb 1999 08:32:22 -0500
X-MSMail-Priority: Normal
X-Mailer: Microsoft Internet Mail 4.70.1162

Mr. Hannon:

Thank you for your interest in our company, The York Consulting Team, Inc. We would be more than happy for you to link to our Web page and use the information in your book with the appropriate credit given to us. When your book is published, please let us know so that we may obtain a copy. If you have any further questions, please don't hesitate to e-mail us.

Sincerely,

Sutton Bennett
Executive Assistant

Neal Hannon wrote:

> Dear Yorkteam,
>
> I am developing material for a new supplement to managerial accounting
> textbooks and have found your wonderful Web site. My focus for the
> proposed book is to present management accounting from the perspective of
> the 70 percent of a real management accountant's job, namely communication,
> teamwork, and using Internet technology to get work done. I find your
> Web site aligned with these objectives.
>
> Thank you for your consideration.
>
> Neal Hannon

E-mail cannot take the place of face-to-face discussions. However, in some circumstances, such as employees that are separated by large distances and time zones, e-mail can provide a valuable and lasting record of electronic exchange. E-mail is normally stored on dedicated computers called servers. Backup of e-mail files are routinely made at the server. This means that even though a person may have read and discarded e-mail, a record of the message may still be recovered from a backup file. E-mail should be written in such a way that everyone who reads the message will understand the intent of the writer.

Business e-mail belongs to the company. A business e-mail address should be only used for company purposes and contain information that any systems administrator or manager could read. Recent court decisions have upheld the right for companies to collect and review e-mail written by company employees. This means that if your e-mail message is not suitable to be read by company officials, revise your message until it is suitable.

### *Voice Mail Messages*

In most businesses, when a person is not available to take a phone call, the caller is given the option to leave a voice mail message. Voice mail records a short message from the caller, giving details about what the person wants to communicate. Most voice mail machines, however, have storage space for only very short messages. Therefore, a voice mail message needs to be short, clear, and contain relevant information.

To ensure a timely response, leave your name and a brief message stating clearly why you want the party to return your call. Remember to leave your phone number as the last part of your message and to speak slowly and clearly. The reason for leaving your phone number at the end of the message is that most voice mail machines give the listener the option to replay the last eight seconds of the message only. Therefore, if the name and phone number are repeated at the end of the message, the listener will not have to play the entire message in order to respond.

### *Speaking to an Audience*

One of the keys to becoming a great communicator is the ability to speak in front of audiences. Presenting a clear message to an audience is a talent that anyone can develop as long as they follow a few basic principles. Good public speakers have a central message to deliver, a proven method of delivery, and good contact with the audience. Each piece of the puzzle contributes to a great presentation.

#### Central Message

Each time a speaker begins, he or she must have a clear idea of what they want the audience to remember. The central message or point of the talk needs to be established in a three-step process. First, tell the audience what you are going to tell them. Second, give them enough details so that they will understand what your message is. Finally, review and remind your audience again what your central message was.

Delivery: Focus on Audience

Effective communication needs to be focused upon the needs of the audience. Each thought or idea presented should contribute to helping the reader of the communication understand something better or be better informed about a topic. Poor communication is generally unclear or off-target with the needs of the recipient.

Additionally, eye contact is very important during delivery. Each person in the audience expects you to look directly at them at least once every 5 to 10 minutes. This technique helps obtain, hold, and sustain interest. It also serves as feedback to the speaker about how much of the information is being absorbed. People who are turning their heads away or talking to their neighbors are not engaged in the presentation.

Review

The best was to make sure your audience will remember your message is to repeat the message during your close. Good speakers will prime the audience that the close is near with definite verbal clues. Once the audience is expecting the close, deliver the summary of the central message.

**Exercise**

1) Develop an outline for a 15-minute talk on the importance of determining the correct activities to drive activity-based costs.

______________________________________________

______________________________________________

______________________________________________

______________________________________________

______________________________________________

2) What is the central message of your talk?

______________________________________________

______________________________________________

______________________________________________

______________________________________________

______________________________________________

## *Delivering Financial Information in Written Reports*

Financial information often needs to be displayed in written reports. At first glance, the placing of financial information within a report seems as easy as cut and paste. The problem, however, is to come up with words that help the reader understand what is happening in the business. For example, the narrative for a monthly financial report should highlight the major deviations from the business plan both on the positive and the negative side. The numbers do not speak for themselves.

**Exercise**

Using the following Providence Mutual Fund Report, create a monthly report that helps explain the major deviations from plan. Although in a normal business situation you would be required to research the actual reasons for the deviations to plan, in this exercise you will be allowed to make your own reasonable assumptions for the numbers.

**Providence Mutual Fund**
**Monthly Activity Report - Growth Sector**
**Month Ending December, 2001**

| Activity | Monthly Activity | Budget | Cost | Bud-Cost |
|---|---|---|---|---|
| Processing new accounts | 345 | 32,000 | 20,650 | 11,350 |
| Mailing prospectuses | 933 | 12,000 | 10,350 | 1,650 |
| Processing monthly stock rpts. | 24,352 | 2,200,000 | 2,191,680 | 8,320 |
| Filing SEC registration materials | 9 | 12,000 | 15,687 | (3,687) |
| Training | 14 | 9,000 | 10,200 | (1,200) |
| Phone requests | 4,860 | 378,000 | 437,400 | (59,400) |
| Personal/sick/vacation time | 45 | 125,000 | 129,600 | (4,600) |
| Closing old accounts | 8,565 | 150,000 | 342,600 | (192,600) |
| Mailing checks | 9,388 | 21,500 | 37,552 | (16,052) |
| | | 2,939,500 | 3,195,719 | (256,219) |

**Exercise**

Read "What is Activity-Based Costing" by Chris Pieper, located at http://www.abctech.com/univ/execbrf.htm. Write two different 200-word essays about the reasons companies are adapting activity-based costing and why calculating accurate costs are so important to companies today. Each essay should clearly focus on the needs of the intended readers of the essays.

1. The first essay should be written from the point of view of a management accountant writing an informational memo to his or her departmental boss.

2. The second essay should be written from the point of view of a salesperson working for a major software company. It should be written to the chief executive officer of a company who would benefit from purchasing ABC software.

**Exercise**

Compose an e-mail to a group of three classmates organizing an initial meeting for a group project. Remember to be brief, factual, and request that each recipient reply to your message.

**Exercise**

Respond to the following e-mail message with a reply to the sender.

Reply To:
From:
Subject:

>TO: Budget Department
>Subject: Meeting on 10/23 to discuss budget overrun
>From: Susan Overbudget
>
>Terry and I plan to attend the meeting on the 23rd to discuss our departmental overruns on the budget.
>What information should we bring to the meeting? Will the meeting be in meeting room #3 at 10:00 AM?
>Who is expected to attend from the budget department?
>
>Susan

Note: E-mail messages are automatically dated.

# Analytical Skills

Analytical skills are defined as the ability of people to calculate, interpret, and communicate financial information. Businesses of all types need people who have the ability to make sense out of the financial information. Good decision making depends on a good grasp of the facts at hand, with special emphasis on the potential profitability of a possible business direction.

## *Patterns*

When presented with financial information for a given period, the most common question is What do they mean? In other words, what do the numbers say about the health and direction of the business? The answer to the questions depends on many things. First, how do the numbers compare with the prior period? Are the numbers getting better or worse? Second, once the current situation is understood, what can be done in the future to improve the numbers in the next reporting period? Good analytical skills will provide management the direction they need to move forward.

Finding patterns of spending is relatively easy. Are the numbers trending up or down? What are the factors driving the spending? Is the increase or decrease due to volume or activity? The answer to these questions could lead to decisions that will either change the pattern of spending or continue the trend. Spotting when a trend is out of line compared to the activity is a demonstration of analytical skill.

### Exercise

Using the following report, create a 150-word report that analyzes the changes in the reported activities.

**Providence Mutual Fund**
**Monthly Activity Report - Growth Sector**
**Four Months Ending March, 2002**

| Activity | Dec. | Jan. | Feb. | Mar. |
|---|---|---|---|---|
| Processing new accounts | 345 | 352 | 361 | 392 |
| Mailing prospectuses | 933 | 1,002 | 1,100 | 1,213 |
| Processing monthly stock rpts. | 24,352 | 24,933 | 23,987 | 24,852 |
| Filing SEC registration materials | 9 | - | - | 10 |
| Training | 14 | 25 | 12 | 28 |
| Phone requests | 4,860 | 5,213 | 5,311 | 5,599 |
| Personal/sick/vacation time | 45 | 52 | 46 | 82 |
| Closing old accounts | 8,565 | 7,301 | 6,200 | 5,342 |
| Mailing checks | 9,388 | 8,345 | 7,320 | 6,052 |